VALENCIA LAND OF WINE:
A WINEMAKER'S SELECTION

Valencia Land of Wine:
A Winemaker's Selection

Joan C. Martín

Published by Anaconda Editions, 2007
© Anaconda Editions

British Library Cataloguing-in-Publication Data
A catalogue record for this book is available from the British Library

ISBN 978 1 901990 04 1

Anaconda Editions
84 St Paul's Crescent
London NW1 9XZ
email: anaconda@winesofvalencia.com

Per Amparo i Virginia, dues companyes excepcionals, per tot l'amor i la seva generosa devoció.

For Amparo and Virginia, two exceptional companions, for all their love and unstinting devotion.

Contents

Foreword

I sometimes wonder whether wine from the Valencia region really exists. A guide to Spanish wine published in Madrid in 2005 included the following regions in its table of contents: Jeréz (sherry), Rioja, Ribera del Duero, Priorato, Toro, Rías Baixas, Bierzo, Mallorca and Murcia. The only reference to the wines of the Comunidad Valenciana came under the general heading "Vinos de España". It amounted to no more than a passing reference to "The enormous potential shown by the wines of Utiel-Requena." That was it. The rest was silence. Is the author ignorant or are the wines of the Valencia region routinely overlooked? Probably both. However, wine from the **Comunidad Valenciana** was among the first to circumnavigate the globe. Ferdinand Magellan, a Portuguese seaman in the service of the Spanish crown, ordered 200 casks of the renowned, long-lasting, oxidized "rancio de Alicante" before beginning his colossal undertaking. And this same **Fondillón** from Alicante graced the captains' tables of the Royal Navy, just as it rounded off meals at royal banquets across the courts of Europe, and appeared as an ingredient in the most exalted recipe books. For many years this wine from Alicante was held in great prestige throughout Europe, hence the references in such classics as Alexandre Dumas's *The Count of Montecristo*, in which **Fondillón** (or "Alicante") is commended as the perfect accompaniment to a biscuit (see page 52).

The phylloxera epidemic did for **Fondillón** and with it the renown of wine from the País Valencià. Winemaking entered into a long period of decline. Once the trauma of the wine plague was over, the whole chain of production had become geared towards quantity rather than quality. The wineries made gut-rot "vino de pasto" that was undrinkable unless mixed with "gaseosa" lemonade to dilute the harsh taste and the high alcohol content. It ought to be said in defence of the producers and wine merchants of the **Comunitat Valenciana** that in this they were no different from their counterparts along the whole western Mediterranean seaboard from Murcia to Priorato. It is just that in these other areas they moved on from a wine trade based on the bulk production so dear to Valencians in favour of the exploration of new possibilities. They carried out research, innovated, recovered neglected varietals, introduced modern techniques and entered the marketplace with a distinctive high-quality product. Meanwhile, Valencian bodegas were still weighing and buying grapes by the ton.

It was the late 1960s and 1970s before the first bashful, timid, stammering murmurs in the Valencian wine world could be detected. And it is no accident that it was in 1981 that Joan C. Martín, the author of this book, published his first article speaking up for Valencian wine. This was at a time when the wines of Rioja were held in reverent esteem, when Ribera del Duero was still unknown, when French wine cost an arm and a leg, whatever its quality, and Valencian wine was despised by mere dint of its supposedly lowly origin. It was against this background, against the grain, like some sort of benign prophet, armed only with his pen, his convictions and an insuperable faith in the possibilities of his own land that this man of vision came along and, in the manner of a hero in one of his beloved John Ford westerns, announced: "My name is Joan C. Martin, I make wine." Though unlike, say, John Wayne's Sean "Trooper" Thornton in Ford's "The Quiet Man", who arrives fleeing from his own self and demons in his past, Joan was intent on staying in Valencia because his own land is also his dreamland, to him what the "Lake Isle of Innisfree" was to another of his heroes, W.B. Yeats.

I have known Joan Martín for the best part of thirty years. We have a shared taste for good wine, dry martinis, good food, the Havana cigars that – alas – they no longer let me smoke, malt whisky, good conversation, literature and a love for this land that in his case amounts to a passion, and in mine is more chastened and sceptical. It has been said of him that he is the leading voice of the wines of the Valencia region (which he is), an anatomist of the senses (certainly), a winemaking philosopher (that too) and more than just a writer. All of the above is true, and I can vouch for it. But more than that, he is an honest person and a fighter convinced of the fact that rights and victories are rarely conceded, but need to be won. He has been fighting since 1981, spreading the word about Valencian wine in books such as Joan Piqueras' *Els vins valencians* (Universitat de València, 1983) and the *Anuario del vino español* (Editorial Sucro, 1984). He is the author of *Manual de vinos valencianos* (José Huguet, 1986) and of *Vinos de las D.O. de la Comunidad Valenciana* (ICEX, 1988), published by the Ministerio de Economía y Comercio in French, English and German.

We have here another book, a collection of articles published in the summers of 2004 and 2005 in the **Comunidad Valenciana** edition of *El País*. It is certainly the most comprehensive work on the wines of the Valencia region available today; but it is far from being just a catalogue of names. Running through this collection there is a seam of erudition, philosophy and literary taste, which takes us on a journey of discovery by means of the wines of the País Valenciano – so little known, so overlooked, so neglected by those very people who should have been their principal advocates, particularly the Valencian government. It is a characteristic paradox that this book should first appear in English rather than in Spanish or Valencian. It has been said that whom the gods wish to destroy they first make blind, and the governing politicians of Valencia have been and remain either very blind or at least wilfully looking the other way.

But let us turn to the book in hand. This collection would not have been possible without *El País* newspaper, without the knowledge of its author and without the enthusiasm of its editor at Anaconda Editions, John Maher, who in his quest for information on Valencian wine came – inevitably – across Joan Martín. The two "Juanes" share a passion for wine and for Ireland, a firm foundation for an impregnable partnership. Cicero said something along the lines of men being like wine, time sours the bad and improves the good. Joan C. Martín is one of the good guys. And this book, which should be read with a good glass of **Comunidad Valenciana** wine to hand, is also a good thing.

Let us raise our glasses to the enjoyment of both.

Josep Torrent
Editor
El País, Comunidad Valenciana edition

Editor's Preface

It was like striking gold when I came across Joan C. Martín's articles on wines from the Valencia region on the *El País* website. I had been on a fruitless quest for useful information on the wines of the three **Denominaciones de Origen** of the **Comunidad Valenciana** (**DO** Alicante, **DO** Utiel-Requena and **DO** Valencia) since moving to the city of Valencia in 2006. What few references to the subject I had managed to find bore scant relation to the excellence and remarkable variety of the wines I was buying locally. Here were cheerful sparkling Moscatels and Cavas, white wines from international varieties such as Chardonnay and Sauvignon Blanc, as well as the local Merseguera, Macabeo and others, similarly rosés and reds of intense colour and flavour from Cabernet Sauvignon, Syrah, Tempranillo, as well as Monastrell and Bobal from the region. Then there was a perplexing array of sweet wines, "**Mistelas**" alongside other delicately succulent styles of Moscatel, not to mention the unique and ancient **Fondillón** from Alicante. It was clear that there was a boom in the wines of the **Comunidad Valenciana** to rival the construction fever busily destroying the region's coastline. Yet I could find no one to turn to for advice or information on the subject. A look of panic-stricken perplexity crossed the faces of the otherwise helpful people at the local Tourist Offices whenever I casually enquired whether they had any information about the region's wines. Nor were waiters and wine lists particularly forthcoming.

After reading the *El País* articles I knew I had to meet Joan. I called the paper's Valencia offices, where with characteristically Valencian generosity of spirit I was put straight through to his mobile phone. I left a garbled message, and Joan, in what I was to learn was a promptness possibly born of his time in the Spanish marines, called me back and we arranged to meet. I had seen several references to Ireland in Joan's writings, and my Irish background helped forge an immediate bond.

Joan's encyclopaedic knowledge of wine in general and Valencian wine in particular is underpinned by the fact that he is both winemaker and wine writer. He has been making wine for even longer than he has been writing about it, even though in January 2007 a gala in his honour was held in recognition of his first twenty-five years writing about the wines of the region. He made the region's first barrel-aged white wine, its first carbonic **maceration** red wine and its first Cava Brut Nature Millésimé (special vintage), before setting up a pioneering bodega committed to making fine wine in the **DO** Valencia, the Companyia Valenciana de Vins i Espirituosos, whose 1994 Millennium Cordial Gran Reserva made from Tempranillo and the local Garnacha Tintorera showed that the sky was the limit for those committed to making the best possible wine.

As readers of this book will discover, Joan Martín is not interested in giving wines points out of 100, or even in providing complex tasting notes. He concentrates on how the wine is made, where it is made and why it is made. The same passionate enthusiasm that he brings to the wines and their places of origin also gives rise to a range of literary reference that is perhaps unfashionable in the more technically-minded and prosaic contemporary English wine-writing style. I find it refreshing and stimulating, both as reader and translator, and I learned a great deal while tracking down the references, from ancient Greece to Gramsci. Although this book is intended as a practical guide, it should be remembered that some time has passed since the articles were first written, and the specific vintages will not always be just as they were at the time of writing (or still being made in the case of a couple of the wines). The book aims to lead the reader into the world of wine from the País Valencià, and there could be no better person to show the way than Joan C. Martín.

To finish, a word about the translation and the text. The names of grape varieties have been kept in Spanish throughout, so we have Garnacha rather than Grenache, Moscatel rather than Muscat, Monastrell rather than Mourvèdre, and so on. A glossary of terms (Spanish, Valencian and wine-related) has been included, and words in the glossary are in bold type in the text, as are references to wines from bodegas mentioned elsewhere in the book. The temptation to include footnotes proved irresistible, a reflection on the range of literary and other allusions in the collection and how much I learned while preparing it for publication. Finally, I should like to thank the Consejos Reguladores of the three **DOs**, Alicante, Utiel-Requena and Valencia, as well as the many individuals and bodegas (and their fine product) that helped the book on its way, particularly Josep Torrent, editor of the **Comunidad Valenciana** edition of *El País*, for commissioning the articles originally and for kindly allowing Anaconda Editions to translate them and publish them in English.

John Maher
Editor and translator
Anaconda Editions and winesofvalencia.com

XV

Glossary

Alquería – a farmhouse and its surrounding land.

Barrel-fermented – the process of fermenting wines in small barrels instead of large vats or stainless steel tanks.

Casa Rural – holiday country cottage.

Comarca – often translated as "county" or "shire"; here it is a traditional locality with no administrative competences, legally referred to as a "homologated territorial demarcation".

Comunidad Valenciana/Comunitat Valenciana – the official name for the Valencia region, encompassing three provinces (Alicante, Valencia and Castellón).

Crianza (see also **Reserva** and **Gran Reserva**) – some slight variations in different regions of Spain, but generally it means the wine has spent at least six months in oak casks and twelve months in bottle.

Denominación de Origen (DO) – wine (and also food) area governed by its own regulatory board to protect quality; **DO** wines must observe regulations which cover all aspects of planting, cultivating, harvesting, vinifying and ageing.

Finca – estate.

Fondillón – A unique unfortified Monastrell-based "rancio" (oxidized or maderized) Alicante wine, aged in large barrels for at least eight years and often over twenty. A wine with 500 years of written history behind it.

Garnacha Tintorera (also known as "Alicante" or just as "Tintorera") – a variant Garnacha found in the Valencia region, with unusually red flesh, if managed well it gives exceptional fruit quality.

Generalitat/Generalitat Valenciana – the regional government of the **Comunidad Valenciana**.

Gran Reserva (see also **Crianza and Reserva**) – wine that spends a minimum 2 years in oak and a further 3 years in bottle for reds. For whites and rosés, the wine must be at least 4 years old and have spent a minimum of 6 months in oak barrels.

Hectare – is a unit of area equal to 10,000 square metres.

Huerta – Market garden, but generally used to refer to the irrigated areas used for cultivation around the city of Valencia (and formerly Alicante).

Maceration – grapes (usually red) crushed and steeped in their juice for days or weeks before, during, or after fermentation.

Mistela (see also **vino de licor, Moscatel de Valencia**, and **vin doux naturel**) – sweet wines (almost always made from Moscatel in the

Valencia region) made by adding grape spirit to non- or partly-fermented wine, which stops the fermentation process while there is still considerable sugar present.

Reserva (see also **Crianza** and **Gran Reserva**) – wine (for reds) that must spend at least 12 months in oak casks and 24 months in bottle. For whites and rosés (much rarer), the wine must be at least 2 years old and have spent a minimum of 6 months in cask.

Riojitis – a nasty and widespread affliction, rendering sufferers incapable of appreciating any wine from outside Rioja.

Riu-Rau – a typical old farmhouse in La Marina Alta with columned porticos for drying grapes.

Second-grade cooperative – a cooperative of cooperatives, in which various smaller outfits are incorporated into a larger one.

Solera system – a series of barrels of the same wine of differing ages, the older ones being nourished by the new wines each year. The wines are aged together to marry the flavours and add complexity.

Subzone – There are four subzones to the Valencia **DO**, each with a distinct character and tradition: Alto Turia, Valentino, Moscatel de Valencia and Clariano.

Vino de (alta) expresión – working term used to describe the concept of producing big, intense, fruit-driven, high-alcohol wines that stress the uniqueness of the designated vineyards or terroir.

Vino de autor – "signature wine", a wine that expresses the characteristic qualities of the winemaker.

Vin doux naturel (vino dulce natural) – though the term translates as "naturally sweet wine", this is not as straightforward as it seems. With "**vins doux naturels**" fermentation is halted by the addition of alcohol killing the yeast, resulting in what is really a blend of wine, unfermented grape juice and added grape spirit. Generally speaking, with **Mistelas** and **vinos de licor**, no fermentation takes place and with **vins doux naturels** there is some fermentation before the addition of spirit.

Vino joven – wine with little or no aging in oak casks.

Vino de licor – see **Mistela**

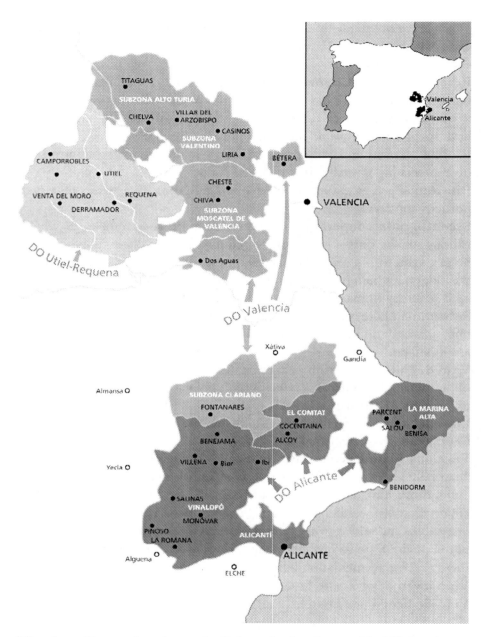

The three Denominaciones de Origen in the Comunidad Valenciana:
DO Alicante (showing Vinalopó, Alicantí, El Comtat and La Marina Alta)
DO Utiel-Requena
DO Valencia (showing subzones Alto Turia, Valentino, Moscatel de Valencia and Clariano)

O for a beaker full of the warm South!
 Full of the true, the blushful Hippocrene,
  With beaded bubbles winking at the brim,

  John Keats, "Ode to a Nightningale"

Al Muvedre:
St [T]elmo's fire
Vinos Telmo Rodríguez, Monòver (DO Alicante)

It should have been a sign to the whole wine world when a bodega from Rioja, and none other than one belonging to the celebrated Telmo Rodríguez,[1] set about making a red Monastrell in the heart of the Alicante **Denominación de Origen** (DO). Telmo is considered one of the best winemakers in the world. In 2005 the Ministry of Trade appointed him, alongside Ferran Adriá, Juan Mari Arzak and other renowned chefs, to lead the worldwide campaign promoting Spanish cuisine and, in his case, wines. The soil and the climate, and the style of wines, are totally different in Alicante and Rioja. The behaviour of the grapes during the winemaking is as different as English ham and Spanish "jamón". Telmo brought in Salvador Poveda Martínez, a young winemaker from a long-established wine dynasty in Monòver in the Vinalopó area of Alicante (see page 52), to oversee the production and development of the wine. His grandfather, Salvador Poveda Luz, was one of the great winemakers of the País Valenciano, rescuer of the legendary **Fondillón** and maker of remarkable reds such as Doble Capa, which was ahead of its time and one of the best wines ever to be produced on the whole Mediterranean seaboard. In its day this wine got the highest marks year after year in the lists of Spain's finest wines from such authorities as the Club del Gourmet, José Peñín and Xavier Domingo.

When Telmo met the young winemaker, he knew that he would be a star. After studying at the Escuela de Viticultura y Enología de Requena (henceforth Requena Wine School) under teachers like Pedro Navarro, Francisco Gabaldón, Félix Cuartero and Félix Jiménez, Salvador displayed his winemaking culture, the basis of every good winemaker. In his family's bodega he learnt the secrets of the trade from his father and his uncle, as well as the mysteries of Monastrell, a generous but demanding grape. His **Al Muvedre** is 100 percent Monastrell and a hefty, but easy-drinking, 14.5% ABV. It is almost vermilion in colour, though with lighter highlights. Its aroma is pure and manages impossibly to combine density and freshness. It is very clean on the nose with a straightforward bouquet of Monastrell itself, alongside sensual hints of ripe wild fruit. It is in the mouth that it really reveals itself as a wine that has achieved magnificence, with a lovely balance between palate and aroma, not like some wines that have a great nose but let you down flat when you taste them, which is pretty much the worst thing you can say about a wine. **Al Muvedre** (Muvedre evokes Mourvièdre, one of the names for the Monastrell grape) on the other hand, as well as having a full and harmonious bouquet, is magnificent in the mouth. It is an outstanding wine that does credit to its makers and confirms the judgement of those of us who have always believed in Monastrell, with its clean and elegant taste of sweet tannins born of ripe fruit, so admirable and elegant that it subtly reminds you of the wine you have just been drinking. All hail to this **Al Muvedre**, though it will come as a shock to those whose palates have been numbed by the dreaded "**Riojitis**" virus, but this is a "**vino de alta expresión**". The irony of it is that the project has had to come from a prestigious and faraway bodega in Rioja – but then what would life be without irony. But it confirms (in the shape of young Salvador himself) what John le Carré said in *The Honourable Schoolboy*, that time devoted to preparation is never time wasted.

Website: None
Label: Al Muvedre
Type: tinto joven
ABV: 14%
Grape: Monastrell
Approx. Price: €4–5
Bodega: Compañía de Vinos Telmo Rodríguez
Address: C. Siete Infantes de Lara, 5, oficina 1, 16006 Logroño
Tel: 941511128
Fax: 941511131
Email: cia@fer.es

NOTES

[1] Bordeaux-trained Spanish winemaker who describes himself as a "driving" (as opposed to a "flying") winemaker. He established the Compañía de Vinos Telmo Rodríguez in 1994 with the aim of making wine all over Spain, both rediscovering forgotten wines and using modern winemaking techniques to get the best out of traditional wines.

[2] Two superstar Spanish chefs. Ferran Adriá owns the world-famous "El Bulli" (www.elbulli.com) restaurant in Catalonia. Juan Mari Arzak is the owner of Restaurante Arzak (www.arzak.info) in San Sebastian. The author was awarded the Juan Mari Arzak National Prize for Gastronomy and the Media in 2005.

Alto Cuevas:
A Barrel-Aged Rosé
Bodega Covilor, Las Cuevas (DO Utiel-Requena)

At the end of the 1980s the authenticity, class and freshness of the rosé wines produced in Alicante and Utiel-Requena saw them make headway in the marketplace as customers recognized their quality and generosity of spirit. It was the culmination of a lot of hard work supporting these wines. The Cuevas de Utiel cooperative was a pioneer in the field with Añal, a Bobal rosé, which was youthful, zesty and full of fruit, and led the way for their range of bottled wines (reds from Tempranillo, and a white Macabeo) – like many regional producers they had previously been bulk sellers of wine. Utiel-Requena has always been notable for the intensity of its Tempranillos, due to its height above sea-level and climate. In the lower part the Bobal reds have worked best, much as they say about Sherry ("pa finos el Puerto y pa olorosos Jeré" – for finos the Puerto [Sanlúcar de Barrameda] and for Olorosos Jeréz [Andalusians tend to drop the final consonant]). A huge marketing drive saw rosés become a popular summer drink up to 1995. That year saw a boom in red wine. Reports of the health benefits of red wine led to a dramatic increase in sales, unfortunately to the detriment of rosé. The response of local bodegas and wine authorities was unintelligent and haphazard. They failed to harness their know-how in the production of rosé wine when they turned to making "**alta expresión**" reds, and there was no promotion campaign to speak of, as they overlooked the individuals behind the successful promotion of the area's rosés. This is characteristic of a business full of self-satisfied blowhards, all too ready to ignore those who have laboured on their behalf. An example of an intelligent response to the fall in sales was **Alto Cuevas' barrel-fermented** rosé, developed by Antonio Gómez, professor and director of studies at the Requena Wine School. Antonio comes from the Vinalopó (specifically, Asp), and although his family grows table grapes he has fully absorbed his locality's rosé tradition. The result of this undertaking at **Las Cuevas** cooperative is a magnificent rosé. **Alto Cuevas** is fermented in new oak barrels after the must has been separated from the grape skins, and has the fresh, fruity, fragrant raspberry and strawberry scent of young red wine. It is noticeably rich in the mouth, with well-balanced fruit and acidity, and round, mature tannins from the wood. A delightful wine, which ought to be served cold. As Robert Burns (who has also given his name to a cigar) urged in "The Toast":

Fill me with the rosy wine,
Call a toast, a toast divine:
Giveth me Poet's darling flame

Website: www.bodegascovilor.com
Label: Alto Cuevas 2002
Type: barrel-fermented rosé
ABV: 12%
Grape: Bobal
Approx. price: €2–3
Bodega: COVILOR (Coop. Agrícola Valenciana "Virgen de Loreto")
Address: C/ Nuestra Sra. de Loreto, 17, 46313 Cuevas de Utiel, Valencia
Tel: 962182053
Fax: 962182055
Email: oficina@bodegascovilor.com

Aula:
Four of a Kind
Coviñas, Requena (DO Utiel-Requena)

In the Utiel-Requena **DO**, the **second-grade cooperative Coviñas** takes in more grapes than any other winery in the area. It incorporates various cooperatives in Requena and some from other localities. Founded in 1965 to overcome the barriers that impeded commercial development and the generation of a decent revenue, **Coviñas** achieved its social and economic objectives to a greater extent than its winemaking ones. The cooperative and its wines have been almost Gramscian in their approach.[1] This is perhaps due to the social and political character of some of the participating cooperatives, such as Valenciana de Viticultores, founded in 1937 in the wave of voluntary collectivizations that might – if the Republic had won the Civil War – have seen many Valencian pueblos become cooperative communities along the lines of Israel's moshavim and kibbutzim, which have been of such human and economic benefit to that country.

But life and economics go on, and once the basics had been put in place **Coviñas** began its great leap forward with modern management and a business approach that positioned its wines effectively in the marketplace. Today it sells over five million bottles of quality wine in the European Union, Switzerland, the Asian Pacific and North America. Not bad for an operation that began with the motto that "a kilo is a kilo" and that every grape grown should be harvested and that everything harvested should be made into wine. The driving force behind the success of **Coviñas** wines has been its leadership and team spirit – not always the case with cooperatives as members tend to overestimate their business abilities, and invariably think that they could do better than the professionals they have brought in, often leading to commercial and economic difficulties. **Coviñas** was one of the first bodegas to make quality wine, over twenty-five years ago, in the shape of the first version of today's ubiquitous **Enterizo**, originally called Vino de la Reina. I prefer the name **Enterizo**, which is more real than Reina, more everyday, more Gramscian. In Spanish **Enterizo** means "of a single piece", which can be applied to a wine, or anything that is whole and seamless, "one-piece". Nowadays, their **Enterizo** wines (red, white and rosé) are not as distinguished, though they remain very good. The difference is one of degree.

Then they made some tens of thousands of bottles, now they make millions. The best **Coviñas** wines are the four wines in the **Aula** range, of limited production in which the interplay of grape varieties is the management's strong suit. Here we can see the hand of a fine professional, Rafael Orozco, from La Manchuela just over the Valencia border in Albacete, who has become a Valencian through and through. He is a technician who approaches winemaking with German precision and French elegance. The best wine in the **Aula** range is their Syrah **crianza** 2002. What an interesting wine and what wonderful wood from the barrels! There is a touch of the old **Enterizo** (anyone who remembers it will know what I mean) in this **Aula Syrah**, in the depth of its tannins, that taste of wild truffles, the rather smoky aroma. **Aula** has another virtue, it is a wine that will last for a long time, worth buying now and following its development. It is excellent value, and is a well-made product, the fruit of hard-working professionals. Every time I come across a good pro like Orozco, I am reminded of a scene in the film "The Remains of the Day", where one of the pre-World War II powerbroker characters, in defending the rights of ordinary people, pays homage to the professionals of this world (as embodied in the butler played by Anthony Hopkins), "You need professionals to run your affairs, or you're headed for disaster!"

Website: www.covinas.com
Label: Aula Syrah 2002
Type: tinto crianza
ABV: 13%
Grape: Syrah
Approx. price: €6–8
Bodega: Coviñas
Address: Avda. Rafael Duyos, s/n, 46340 Requena, Valencia
Tel: 962301469
Fax: 962302651
Email: covinas@covinas.com

NOTES

[1] Antonio Gramsci (1891–1937) was an important Italian Marxist and political theorist, who among other things stressed the importance of the cultural dimension in the political sphere.

Bárbara Grial:
Good For Alto Turia
Covibex, Alto Turia (DO Valencia)

La Serranía is the main winegrowing area in the Alto Turia **subzone** of the Valencia **DO**, producing almost four million kilos of grapes from 1,142 **hectares** under vine. It is mountain winegrowing in its purest form. The Tuéjar and Turia rivers run across it in deep and tortuous gorges and there are steep slopes on which the Merseguera grape is cultivated. There is a certain similarity to the Upper Middle Rhine above Koblenz, such as Drachenfels (where Siegfried did battle with the dragon in the Song of the Nibelungs). In the Alto Turia, the landscape, the climate and the grape variety have combined to produce an excellent and singular white wine. When the recovery of Valencian wine was getting under way, the Alto Turia pioneered bottles of fresh and fruity white wines. But if the Alto Turia amounts to anything today, it is due to men such as José Torres Ruiz, one of those rare Valencian big-hearted, civic-minded figures, who give while asking for nothing in return and disappear before their time without anyone thanking them for what they have done. José Torres studied at the Requena Wine School under Pascual Carrión, the father figure of modern Valencian wine, where he was imbued with a love of wine and of his country as well as technical know-how.

But the development of Alto Turia slowed in recent years. Though there is hope for the future, and the area has grown with the incorporation of the Calles locality, where the ultramodern Vegamar bodega has been set up next to the River Tuéjar. This is an excellent development, as the area urgently needed new capital and ideas to move forward. Another initiative that improved the quality of these wines was the establishment of the **second-grade Covibex cooperative** to improve production and trade in the towns of Valdobar and Los Campos. They use their Merseguera grapes to make **Bárbara Grial**, a refined, perfumed and very lively white wine. This is a very distinctive modern wine, with a touch of wildness, as if the mountains had contributed something of their character. The same character that St Vincent Ferrer invoked in his sermon "Vosaltres de la Serrania",[1] and Richard Ford described in his *Handbook for Travellers in Spain*.[2] The inhabitants – winegrowers or otherwise – of La Serranía will need to call on that character to defend the heritage of their locality, which belongs in turn to all Valencians. One of the underlying causes of the Alto Turia's wine difficulties has been the devastation of the area — quarries and frenzied construction make uncomfortable bedfellows for good wine. If there is no countryside left there can be no good modern wine either.

Website: www.anecoop.com
Label: Bárbara Grial 2004
Type: blanco joven
ABV: 11.5%
Grape: Merseguera
Approx. price: €3
Bodega: Covibex
Address: Carretera N-III km 314, 46370 Chiva, Valencia
Tel: 962522200
Fax: 962522678
Email: covibex@covibex.com

NOTES

[1] Sant Vicent Ferrer, *Reportationes sermonum Reueredissimi Magistri Vicentii Ferrarii, predicatoris finis mundi* (1412–18), "Vosaltres de la Serrania qui estats enmig de Castella e de Catalunya, e per ço prenets algun vocable castellà e altre català. La nostra vida és el mig: dessús és la glòria e dejús infern." ("You people of the Serrania, halfway between Castile and Catalonia, who for that reason use now a Castilian word and then a Catalan. Our life is the middle: above is the glory and below lies hell.")

[2] Richard Ford (1796–1858) spent the years 1830–34 on riding tours in Spain. A hispanophile, connoisseur and critic (though no admirer of St Vincent, whom he describes as preaching "a crusade of blood and confiscation to a fanatic people"), his *Handbook for Travellers in Spain* (first published 1845) is regarded as one of the finest travel books in the English language. *The Times* declared upon its publication, "So great a literary achievement has never before been performed under so humble a title."

Cañamar Malvasía:
Wine of the Almogavars
La Baronía de Turís, La Ribera Alta (DO Valencia)

Of the six eastern varietals (Muscat of Alexandria, Malvasía, Grenache Blanc, Monastrell, Cabernet Franc and Syrah), three reached Europe through Valencia. Monastrell and Malvasía at the hands of the Almogavars on their return from Byzantium.[1] Ramón Muntaner, one of Roger de Flor's generals and chronicler of the expedition, tells how those battle-hardened fighters had a taste for the wines of Cephalonia, where they had established their headquarters after capturing the citadel of Monemvasia (known as "the Gibraltar of the east"), from which the Malvasía grape derives its name.[2] Many planted these varietals when they returned to their lands in Alicante and Valencia, giving rise to the great Valencian wines of the Renaissance period. Muntaner returned to Valencia in 1307 to marry his betrothed, an heiress from Xirivella who owned a fine "**alquería**". There he planted Malvasía, from where it went to Madeira (hence the Malmsey – a corruption of Malvasía – style of Madeira) and the Canary Islands in the fifteenth and sixteenth centuries. The grape was grown in Xirivella until industrial growth drove it out. As late as 1850, Pascual Madoz in his statistical and geographic dictionary emphasized the town's wine production.[3] From here it passed to Turís, where it is much grown today. Malvasía is an aromatic white grape with intense fruit and sweetness, which lends itself, as in the case of Madeira, to the making of fine dessert wines, since it achieves 15% ABV with 8 grams of residual sugar, ideal for ageing and attaining nobility. The **Turís** cooperative produces **Cañamar** using a "solera" system, with the wine being transferred every three years, though the wine in the **solera** is, of course, older. This cooperative, founded in 1920, produces wines and **Mistelas** in a modern style, though somewhat generic in character. They also make a good, fruity white wine, and one of the best communion wines, **San Leandro** (see page 100). Their best wine of all is **Cañamar**, a sweet, generous and fragrant white made from Malvasía, with aromas of roast coffee beans and spices, with hints of toffee and tobacco in the mouth (as a result of the **solera** ageing). **Cañamar** is a fine digestif, best served in a balloon brandy glass to enhance its fragrance, a wonderful way of rounding off a meal. **Turís** have a neglected treasure in **Cañamar** (it is a steal at the price), and they would be well advised to explore new winemaking techniques in the development of their own distinctive wine-making style. This exists elsewhere – in Madeira they use what is fundamentally a "bain marie" system with a hot water circuit surrounding wine containers. Rounding off a meal with an old wine is the mark of a civilized and cultured person. As de Cassagnac once observed, the order of appearance of wines is the opposite to that of the guests, the most respectable arrive last.[4]

Website: www.baroniadeturis.es
Label: Cañamar
ABV: 15%
Type: oak-aged sweet wine
Grape: Malvasía
Approx. price: €4
Bodega: La Baronía de Turís, Coop. V.
Address: Ctra. Godelleta, 22, 46389 Turís, Valencia
Tel: 962526011
Fax: 962527282
Email: acalvet@baroniadeturis.es

NOTES

[1] From the Arabic "Al-Mugavari" meaning "raider" or "devastator", a type of Aragonese and Catalan soldier prominent during the Christian reconquest of the Iberian peninsula, much employed as mercenaries in Italy and the Middle East during the thirteenth and fourteenth centuries – their name lives on in the modern-day Spanish parachute brigade, "Brigada de Infantería Ligera Paracaidista Almogávares VI".

[2] Ramon Muntaner (1265–1336), soldier and chronicler of the Catalan Company of the East. See Ramon Muntaner, *Chronicle of Muntaner* (Hakluyt Society, 1920), transl. Anne K. Goodenough. Roger de Flor (1267–1305) was a Knight Templar and military adventurer who founded the Catalan Company to fight in the conflict between the Byzantine Empire and the Turks, before eventually being assassinated by the emperor Michael Palaeologus.

[3] Pascual Madoz, *Diccionario geográfico-estadístico-histórico de España y sus posesiones de Ultramar* (P. Madoz y L. Sagasti, 1845–1850).

[4] Paul de Cassagnac wrote *Les Vins de France* (Hachette, 1927).

Carlota Suria:
From Dom Pérignon to Cavafy
Pago de Tharsys, Requena (DO Utiel-Requena)

At the Benedictine abbey at Hautvilliers in Champagne the apocryphal story is told of how a monk, Dom Pierre Pérignon, called to his fellows: "Come quickly, brothers! I'm tasting stars!" on tasting the sparkling wine produced accidentally when a second fermentation occurred in the bottles in the abbey's cellar in spring. The abbey was founded by the Benedictines in 650 AD in the Dark Ages, as a result of Irish monks coming to return the classical culture which had been lost with the fall of Rome at the hands of the Barbarians.

The world was still young and, as Cavafy described in "Waiting for the Barbarians", our own people returned from the border when we expected the Barbarians.[1] As the Irish monks showed when they rescued our civilization, the end depends on the beginning. This must have been what it was like for Vicente García twenty-something years ago, when, as a winemaker for several Cava producers in the Penedès, he and some friends founded a Cava winery in "his Requena".

Vicente García is the man behind **Pago de Tharsys**, his most cherished project, and he has made, as we knew he would, an exquisite Cava: **Carlota Suria Brut Nature**, chosen by Enoforum 2005 (in a blind-tasting by members of the wine trade), as the best Cava in Spain. **Carlota Suria** has tiny bubbles, as after fermenting on their sides in bottle ("en la rima") and being clarified by being inclined on a special rack ("pupitre") it is aged a further fifteen months on its lees. **Carlota Suria** is an elegant dry "nature" (meaning it has from 0 to 3 grams of residual sugar and no addition of reserve wine), with a touch of acidity and a luscious bouquet of salted almonds, making it ideal chilled as an aperitif, although it is a good idea to breathe it in after each sip, and enjoy its scent, like the luxury perfume of a dowager duchess. **Pago de Tharsys** is an all-in-one bodega in which grapes from their own surrounding vineyards are used in making, developing and bottling the wine. It is a model château, the most fully realized in the whole of the País Valenciano, embodying this winemaking philosophy in the same way as the best producers in the Médoc. **Pago de Tharsys** also produces a rarity that is full of Hellenic wisdom: a naturally sweet wine from the Greek grape variety Thomson-Schiller, harvested when the grapes are nearly raisins and producing a very delicate, feminine, milky nectar. Vicente García is endlessly creative, and he has added a "Blanc de Noirs" – a white Cava from the red Bobal grape. Just as Dom Pérignon did when he stumbled on Champagne, in which the predominant grape is Pinot Noir.

I recommend visiting **Pago de Tharsys**, as sacred ground – just like the abbey at Hautvillers with its cellar, its relics of St Helena and tomb of Dom Pérignon, despite the fact that the abbey and its vineyards are a shadow of what they were in the nineteenth century (the result of revolutions and the battles of Verdun and the Marne). The legacy of Dom Pérignon has been wisely followed by Vicente García and other "mestres xampanitzadors", who followed for love of the search itself, as in Cavafy's lines:

> Ithaca has given you the beautiful voyage.
> Without her you would never have set out on the road.

Website: www.pagodetharsys.com
Label: Carlota Suria 2003
Type: Brut Nature
ABV: 11.5%
Grape: Macabeo
Approx. price: €9–10
Bodega: Pago de Tharsys
Address: Paraje de Fuencaliente s/n (Ctra.N-III, Km. 274),
46340 Requena, Valencia
Tel: 962303354
Fax: 962329000
Email: pagodetharsys@pagodetharsys.com

NOTES

[1] Constantine Cavafy (1864–1933), "Waiting for the Barbarians" (1904). The quote at the end of this chapter is from "Ithaca" (1911).

Casa Lo Alto:
The Wine on the Hill
Casa Lo Alto, Venta del Moro (DO Utiel-Requena)

The soil and the contours of **Casa Lo Alto** make it one of the best wine-growing properties in the Comunidad Valenciana. There are 60 **hectares** under vine – comprising Bobal, Garnacha, Tempranillo, Cabernet Sauvignon, Franc, Pinot Noir and Syrah – around the hill ("Lo Alto" – the high place) which gives the place its name, by the houses and the fully-fitted bodega, including two state-of-the-art carbonic maceration containers which were the first to be installed in the Valencia region. The two Swiss winemakers and the "**finca**" manager make a mid-European style wine with a hint of sweetness, thanks to the excellent harmony between the mature tannins of the grapes and those of the barrels, cut with a sharpness that indicates further improvement in the bottle. This is characteristic of central European wines, made with the ripe grapes with their darkened seeds beloved of the winemakers of the Swiss Winemaking Academy, which here has merged with the Utiel-Requena terroir to produce a wine with Mediterranean character and alcohol levels in an ideal blend. Cristóbal Ruiz Ricarte is the creator of this wine, managing a "**finca**" far from its owners (who are C. August Egli AG from Zurich), and also overseeing the pressing of the grapes, the vinification, racking and ageing, as well as working the land, cropping, grafting, pruning and harvesting, embodying Baudelaire"s lines from "L'Âme du vin":

> I know how much was needed on that burning hill
> In painful effort, sweat and how much nurturing sun
> To generate my life and give me soul to fill[1]

Cristóbal is the best winegrower in the País Valenciano, a good man and a wise one (his philosophical utterances are marked by a transparent simplicity). When it comes to wine, the human factor, which unlike the soil and the climate can be chosen, is vital in ensuring that a good wine begins on the vine. This **Casa Lo Alto** red is really a "**reserva**", since it has spent fourteen months in barrel, it is made with 80% Tempranillo, 15% Cabernet Sauvignon, long-haul varietals which provide a sinewy freshness and vigour, and 5% Syrah, whose ripe fullness rounds out the taste. The final balance is achieved by ageing in oak barrels from France's Massif Central, the finer pores of which (1.5 mm on average as against the 2.5 mm of American oak) allow for a very gentle oxidation and improvement in bottle, where that mature bouquet will achieve further refinement and tastes of fruits of the forest (blueberry and raspberry), spice (vanilla and cinnamon), some toast in the aftertaste, and that suggestion of the best butter and redcurrant so characteristic of central European wine.

Website: www.haecky.ch
Label: Casa Lo Alto 2001 crianza
Type: Red crianza
ABV: 14%
Grapes: Tempranillo, Cabernet Sauvignon, Syrah
Approx. price: €15
Bodega: Casa lo Alto
Address: Finca Casa Lo Alto, Ctra. Venta del Moro-Los Isidros, s/n, 46310 Venta del Moro
Tel: 962139101
Email: martin.ruegsegger@haecky.ch

NOTES

[1] Charles Baudelaire, "L'Âme du vin" (The Soul of Wine) in *Les Fleurs du mal* (1857), trans. Peter Dean.

Casta Diva:
Wine of the Sea
Gutiérrez de la Vega, Parcent (DO Alicante)

When Felipe Gutiérrez de la Vega started out in 1980, the wine situation in the **Comunidad Valenciana** was difficult. The idea of making excellent and distinctive wines was for visionaries. Felipe, however, had a great love of wine culture and a cosmopolitan palate. He left the Spanish navy (with the rank of commander) in order to make wine from the vineyards owned by Pilar, his wife, armed with a couple of barriques in a "**riu-rau**" (a typical old farmhouse with columned porticos for grapes to dry in) in Xàbia. The area of La Marina had lost its wine reputation but the Moscatel of Alexandria and the "Giró" (the local name for Garnacha) grapes make excellent wines in France (Beaumes-de-Venise, St-Jean-de-Minervois), Catalonia (Priorat) and California (Napa and San Joaquin valleys). Felipe began by making "**alta expresión**" reds (using the best hand-picked grapes from old vines) with Garnacha, blazing a trail and creating a new range: **Casta Diva** (not that chaste goddesses are such a common phenomenon). Winemaking had moved on from being a craft in the nineteenth century to industrial chemistry and subsequently high technology in the 1970s. The 1990s saw a clinical winemaking replace traditional bodegas with antiseptic installations, and Felipe humanized this, so that technology is used to extract not only the highest quality of fruit, but also the identity of the wine. He has shown this with his red wines, **Viña Ulises** (see page 124) dedicated to Homer and James Joyce, the **Rojo y Negro** dedicated to Stendhal and Dashiell Hammett, and the **Casta Diva Blanco Cosecha Miel** (dedicated to Spain's Nobel prize-winning writer Camilo José Cela and the soprano Montserrat Caballé), a "**vin doux naturel**" Moscatel. The wine was a surprise in the 1980s. The predominant white wine style at the time was light, dry, sharp and cold. **Casta Diva** is the polar opposite: dense, intensely aromatic and sweet. Gastronomes identified its ideal accompaniment: foie gras, as with the great sweet Bordeaux wines from the left bank of the Garonne (Sauternes, Barsac, Cadillac). These are not artificially sweetened wines. **Casta Diva** is made from mature grapes, in contact with a proportion of the skin of the grapes, then matured in oak — 6 months in French oak barrels — where it acquires its exquisite, silky, almond bouquet. **Casta Diva** is the civilized and cosmopolitan creation of a man of the sea who fell in love with wine and a magical wine area. Felipe is master and commander of a movement which has led to the renovation of the region of La Marina and its wines. Enjoy **Casta Diva** with some foie gras from Périgord, a quiche or a lobster bisque. No wonder Camilo José Cela wrote to the winemaker: "They're splendid, delicious and first-rate – your wines, Felipe, are my wines."[1]

Website: www.castadiva.es
Label: Casta Diva Cosecha Miel 2002
Type: Barrel-aged **vin doux naturel**
ABV: 14%
Grape: Moscatel de Alejandría (Muscat of Alexandria)
Approx. price: €15–16 (50 cl)
Bodega: Gutiérrez de la Vega
Address: Canalejas 4, 03792 Parcent, Alicante
Tel: 966405266
Fax: 966405257
Email: info@castadiva.es

NOTES

[1] Camilo José Cela (1916–2002) was a Spanish novelist, travel writer and controversialist. He was awarded the Nobel Prize for Literature in 1989.

Castillo de Chiva Moscatel:
Science and Imagination
Coop. Vínica Chivana, Chiva (DO Valencia)

Every winegrowing area has its own style of wine, both in terms of the vines and the methods of production. So we have a Penedès style, an Albariño and a Mosel style, to name a few white wines. Rafael Michelena, one of the great agricultural engineers and winemakers of these parts, was telling me, wrongly in my view, that we need to develop a distinctive style for the white wines from **DO** Valencia, as with the regions mentioned above. Michelena — as well as being a good, loyal and honest person — is a leading figure in the region's cooperative winemaking, being technical director of the federation of cooperatives, and before that he was technical director of the biggest exporter of Spanish wine. It must be the influence of the incorrect strategies that he has to put up with that prevent him from recognizing that Valencian white wines already have a style and personality of their own, whether they are made solely with Moscatel or whether this grape is blended with other regional grapes, such as the neutral Merseguera or Macabeo. Of the five best white wines in the País Valenciano, four are made wholly or in part with Moscatel (**Casta Diva Cosecha Miel, Viña Teulada, Castillo de Chiva** and **Los Monteros**). The style is very important because it defines the personality and quality of the wine, which as a food product, needs an identity to create a demand. It is not for nothing that Karl Marx said that to know a country one must eat its bread and drink its wine.

Castillo de Chiva dry Moscatel[1] is a very aromatic, light dry white wine, soft and full of fruit, produced by **Bodega Vínica Chivana** in Valencia's equivalent of central Piedmont (La Foia de Bunyol). Here Josep María Furió, winemaker and agricultural engineer, sage and old hand, and for many years a teacher at the Requena Wine School, has successfully developed a very fine "mosto flor" (free-run juice flowing from grapes crushed by their own weight without any mechanical pressing) and a range of modern wines. Furió is one of those agricultural engineers who move on to winemaking, where they apply their science and imagination in practical fashion, and he has done a magnificent job modernizing the wines in this "**comarca**", achieving first-rate white wines and **Mistelas. Vínica Chivana** has 200 winegrowing members producing 2,000,000 kilos of grapes a year, as well as hiding a treasure among its dusty barrels in the cellar, a wonderful old Pedro Ximénez of some 17% ABV. The cooperative also makes an excellent, fragrant and delicate Moscatel **Mistela**. This **Castillo de Chiva Moscatel** has a fruity bouquet (of Moscatel grapes, apricots, peaches) with verdant hints (pine and thyme), and in the mouth it is sweet without being sticky, and served cool it is the height of summer decadence.

Website: www.vinicachivana.com
Label: Castillo de Chiva Muscat seco 2003
Type: Blanco joven
ABV: 12%
Grape: Moscatel de Alejandría
Approx. price: €3
Bodega: Coop. Vínica Chivana
Address: Plaza Aniceto Blasco, s/n, 46370 Chiva, Valencia
Tel: 962520036
Fax: 962520036
Email: bodega@vinicachivana.com

NOTES

[1] The author holds this wine in such high regard that he has written about it twice, in 2004 and again (about the next vintage) in 2005, overleaf.

Castillo de Chiva Dry Moscatel:
Valencia's "Fumé Blanc"
Coop. Vínica Chivana, Chiva (DO Valencia)

When the great Robert Mondavi, one of the best winemakers ever – and the most significant in California since Father Junipero Serra[1] – created his famous Sauvignon Blanc, Napa Valley Fumé Blanc, he was not only making a great wine, he was creating a new style of wine. A style based on varietals with a distinct personality such as Sauvignon Blanc, and leading the way for others like Moscatel or Malvasía, capable of producing similar nutty, smoky tastes.

Moscatel is the white grape that gives personality to the wines of the Valencia **DO**, and in Alicante it is not only used in sweet wines and **Mistelas**, but also for dry and barrel-aged wines like the Moscatel from the **Cooperativa Vínica Chivana**. If Chardonnay is the Burgundy grape par excellence, Macabeo defines the Penedès in Catalonia, as does Verdejo in Rueda, and here it is Moscatel, which plays its part in almost all the whites produced in the region.

This Moscatel from **Vínica Chivana** has spent around 9 months maturing in French oak casks. The result could not be more delightful. It is attractively pale, with touches of amber. On the nose it is aromatic and full of fruit, as you would expect from a wine made from this grape, as scented as the sea breeze. But that sense of smokiness, of fish roe or "mojama" (dried tuna) adds a further touch of distinction. The taste is dry, though with a hint of sweetness and some acidity. It is delicious drunk chilled in all its vivaciousness. It is a quintessentially lively Moscatel. This cooperative produces several good wines such as its red **crianza** and its **Castillo de Chiva Mistela**, and it has some very old Pedro Ximenez with which it could produce earth-shaking wines. Of course, to do all this you need a good winemaking background, which includes a good idea of who any given wine is aimed at, and why. **Vínica Chivana** is an efficient cooperative, one of the best run in Valencia, which has continued to make progress and invest as it goes, in a sustainable way, keeping pace with its market. This is typical of the hard-headed people of the Valencian Piedmont, perhaps because, as W. Woodward used to say, agriculture is not so much a business as a profession.

Vínica Chivana is on the same path as wineries in San Joaquin Valley in Sonoma, California, as depicted in that excellent film "Sideways". And if grape varieties have personalities, as in the ancient fables, Moscatel would surely be the goddess Venus, as in the lines of the Roman poet Terence:[2] "Sine Cerere et Libero friget Venus" ("Without Ceres and Bacchus, Venus would freeze") – in other words, without food and wine, love grows cold.[1] And this Moscatel from the Chivana cooperative should be served chilled, unlike love, which needs its heat.

Website: www.vinicachivana.com
Label: Castillo de Chiva Muscat blanco seco 2004
Type: blanco de crianza
ABV: 11.5%
Grape: Moscatel de Alejandría
Approx. price: €3
Bodega: Coop. Vínica Chivana
Address: Pza. Aniceto Blasco, s/n, 46370 Chiva, Valencia
Tel/Fax: 962520036
Email: bodega@vinicachivana.com

NOTES

[1] The Franciscan missionary Junipero Serra introduced the European grape to southern California in the late eighteenth century..

[2] Publius Terentius Afer (*c.* 185–159 BC), better known as Terence, was a Roman comic poet and playwright.

Castillo de Requena Romeral: The People's Rosé

Romeral Vinícola, Requena (DO Utiel-Requena)

There is much pleasure to be had in unadorned simplicity. One of the most natural and agreeable wines is rosé – real rosé made from red grapes. The Monastrell rosés from Alicante and the Bobal rosés from Utiel-Requena are among the best in the Mediterranean. They are not the only good ones, "clairet" from the Languedoc, the old "clairet" from Sicily and the Sardinian "rojet" have always been held in high esteem at the best tables of this ancient sea. From May to October the heat of the coast, with its rices, "suquets" (fish stewed in its own juices), sauces, fish and seafood, helps turn people's thoughts to rosés rather than reds.

Not long ago I tried a rosé in the Venta l'Home restaurant as an aperitif with some "ajoarriero" (a purée of cod, potato and garlic) that they make better than anywhere else. I followed this with a fine "ventresca" (belly of tuna) and some barbecued rabbit that I had with an Utiel-Requena tinto **crianza** 2001 made from Tempranillo and Cabernet Sauvignon. Perfect food, especially thanks to the rosé, which prepared and brought together my body and my spirit for what followed.

Though rosés can be made from all red grapes, there is a pecking order, and Bobal sits right at the top. Once the grapes are pressed and the must and skins are placed in the deposit, it only takes a few hours to obtain enough colour, aroma and taste for a fine rosé. The tank is then drained and the virgin rosé must is fermented alone. It should be a truly natural wine, like this rosé made by **Romeral Vinícola de Requena**, a medium-sized bodega that buys grapes in the area and makes good whites and even better reds. Their rosé is like fresh juice, natural and agreeably refreshing, with aromas of strawberries and red plums, elegant in the mouth, slightly viscous and with low acidity, or possibly lots as the pleasant fruitiness may be masking it. Anyway, the acidity is not important, as its presence guarantees the freshness of a wine and prolongs the primary aromas (those that come straight from the grape).

This rosé from **Romeral Vinícola** is a straightforward, easy-drinking wine, but as Abraham Lincoln said, "The Lord prefers common-looking people. That is why he made so many of them." Utiel-Requena, with its acres of red Bobal vines, looks like a sea of roses, a wine garden which rustles in the evening east wind. Though consumption of rosé is falling under the onslaught of new style reds, it is a refreshing delight to drink a cool rosé in summertime. Of course, it should be more widely promoted and advertized, and should be supported by the **Generalitat**, as a regional policy, since various localities make this wine and grow the best wines for it. We would be awash with in this wine, which is part of our heritage, if it came from somewhere else. Omar Khayyam, a Persian Muslim, enjoyed a nice rosé in the twelfth century in his own hot climate:

> Wine! That it may have the same pink colour
> as your cheeks; that my regrets
> may be as light.[1]

Website: www.romeralvinicola.com
Label: Castillo de Requena 2004
Type: rosado joven
ABV: 12%
Grape: Bobal
Approx. price: €3
Bodega: Romeral Vinícola
Address: Pol. Ind. El Romeral, 46340 Requena, Valencia
Tel: 962301326
Fax: 962303966
Email: romeral@romeralvinicola.com

NOTES

[1] From the *Rubaiyat* of Omar Khayamm (1048–1123), transl. by Hans van Rossum.

Corolilla Reserva:
The Coronation of Bobal
Bodegas Murviedro, Requena (DO Utiel-Requena)

Bobal is such a rich and varied grape variety that it has yet to fulfil its potential to make different sorts of red wine. Pablo Osorio, the winemaker for **Bodegas Murviedro**, is a consummate technician who, thanks to his know-how and training, has skilfully made two very different Bobal wines, one using **carbonic maceration** and the other being a barrel-aged **reserva**. This grape from the Utiel-Requena **DO** has long had its devotees. I remember how back in 1980 José Vicente Guillén, from the Requena Wine School, proclaimed its qualities and prospects in fundamentalist fashion, as did Claudio Ortiz (a good president of the Utiel-Requena **DO**) and José Alfonso Sierra, the principal technician at the school. Years later, people such as these, with a vision of the future almost on a par with Ireland's W.B. Yeats and Padraig Pearse,[1] now have the satisfaction of seeing their winter turn into spring. Pablo Osorio has achieved a modern **reserva** with his **Corolilla** made from Bobal.

As with the other noble varietals, it is by no means straightforward to make and age a Bobal wine – to make something remarkable requires a remarkable effort. The main difficulty with ageing Bobal is its conductivity. The balance between colour and astringency, residual sugar and overall acidity is very delicate. In barrel the development is slow but also difficult to gauge – the riper the grape, the higher the level of alcohol and colour, but also the greater the level of tannins. Félix Cuartero always advises his students at Requena Wine School not just to keep an eye on the Baume levels (sugar) to decide when to harvest, but also to keep an eye on the seed colour for that moment when they darken from green to brown. It is also true that old Bobal vines produce better-structured and better-balanced wines, but these are less plentiful after the spate of digging up of these vines a decade ago. A great deal of wine heritage was lost, and as Lluis Llach sang, "mal vent que se l'emportà" ("taken by an ill wind").[2]

Corolilla from **Bodegas Murviedro** is a fully realized **reserva** thanks to the fact that Pablo Osorio knows his Bobal, and how to age it in barrel, as the balanced expression of the different qualities of the grape reveals. This is a refined, smooth **reserva**, rounded and structured in the mouth; if you roll it about the palate you will feel the density, but without excessive tannic astringency. One of the most agreeable qualities of this wine is its intense cherry-red colour, filled out by the time in barrel, with flashes of colour reminiscent of Mallorcan tiles. Its very pleasant aroma contains red fruit – plums and redcurrant, on toast – with a touch of balsam. French and American oak barrels have been used, along with the highly intelligent deployment of barrels of Hungarian and Eastern European oak. **Corolilla** is ready to be drunk and enjoyed now, but it will keep a good while, evolving and changing as it goes along, as this grape does.

Website: www.murviedro.es
Label: Corolilla 2000 reserva
Type: Reserva
ABV: 13.5%
Grape: Bobal
Approx. price: €15
Bodega: Murviedro
Address: Ampliación Polígono El Romeral, 46340 Requena, Valencia
Tel: 962329003
Fax: 962329002
Email: murviedro@murviedro.es

NOTES

[1] The long struggle on behalf of the Bobal grape has on occasion brought to mind Pearse's poems "The Rebel":

> I am come of the seed of the people, the people that sorrow;
> That have no treasure but hope,
> No riches laid up but a memory
> Of an Ancient glory.

and "The Mother":

> And tho' I grudge them not, I weary, weary
> Of the long sorrow—And yet I have my joy:
> My sons were faithful, and they fought.

W.B. Yeats' "The Wheel" has the more elegiac, 'Through winter-time we call on spring.'

[2] Lluis Llach is a Catalan singer-songwriter (and latterly winegrower). The quote is from his "L'Estaca" ("The Stake") from 1968, a celebrated parable in the latter years of the Franco dictatorship calling for freedom through united action.

Coto d'Arcis:
Masters of Wine
Bodega Sebirán, Campo Arcís (DO Utiel-Requena)

Campo Arcís is an outpost of Requena where they grow good Bobal and Tempranillo grapes. There is a cooperative, and there is **Bodega Sebirán**, where they make an excellent and remarkable red wine, **Coto d'Arcis Gran Reserva**. Campo Arcís has another virtue, it is the birthplace of the University of Valencia's Professor of Geography, Juan Piqueras, author of one of the best wine studies, *La vid y el vino en el País Valenciano* (Institución Alfonso el Magnánimo, 1980), and who has continued to write fruitfully on the subject. Piqueras can be proud of the progress of his pueblo and of the Bobal grape that he has always supported. The real treasure of Requena lies in its villages, and not in the town, as it is these hamlets dotted throughout the locality that hold its true character.

Coto d'Arcis Gran Reserva 1998 is a red wine made from old vines Bobal along with Tempranillo, Cabernet Sauvignon and Garnacha. This civilized blend is the work of Pedro Navarro, winemaker, and also director of the Requena Wine School. Pedro imparts his wisdom there, as his legendary predecessors Félix Jiménez, Mario Aristo and Pascual Carrión did before him. There's nothing like teaching by example, and Pedro as well as giving his classes at the school, undertook with this bodega to make "**vinos de autor**". As Campo Arcís already has two famous sons (this wine and Professor Piqueras), we might ask if Pedro feels caught between Bacchus and Apollo, between passion and reason. The passion inspired by drinking this dense, mature, warm red, with its exquisite scents of butter and English toffee, the result of blending Cabernet Sauvignon, old vine Bobal and Garnacha, which gives us the classic Cabernet aromas (vanilla and green peppers), but here sitting side by side with something sweet and toasted. The taste is velvety and full, with a good balance of acidity and fruit. After spending the initial months in French and American oak the wine is transferred to barrels of aromatic Portuguese oak.

Coto d'Arcis Gran Reserva is a red wine that is ready for drinking now. **Bodega Sebirán** also produce a **crianza**, a **reserva** from a similar blend and a fresh rosé. All the wines come from their own 92 **hectares** of vineyards. It's all there in the Book of Genesis: "And Noah being an husbandman, went forth and planted a vineyard,"[1] which is very much what Sebirán did, starting with the land, then the vine, and ending up with a bodega. In a village, too!

Website: www.bodegasebiran.com
Label: Coto d'Arcis tinto 1998
Type: Gran reserva
Grapes: Tempranillo, Cabernet Sauvignon, Bobal, Garnacha
ABV: 12.5%
Approx. pice: €10–11
Bodega: Sebirán
Address: C. Perez Galdós, 1, Campo Arcís, 46352 Requena, Valencia
Tel: 962301326
Fax: 962303966
Email: sebiran@tdv.net

NOTES

[1] From David Daniell (ed.), *Tyndale's Old Testament* (Yale UP, 1992), Genesis 9:20.

Coto d'Arcis:
Between Bobal and Bordeaux
Bodega Sebirán, Campo Arcís (DO Utiel-Requena)

As stated above, Pedro Navarro is the head of the Requena Wine School and the winemaker of **Bodega Sebirán** in Campo Arcís. Some years back they made a Bobal from old vines whose elegant bouquet has lingered in many people's memory. It was the first self-proclaimed bottling of old vines Bobal, and its aromas of toffee and rich Irish butter, and that scent of roast coffee that you get when you walk past a shop where they still roast the beans. **Sebirán** is a good bodega with a limited production which is at its best making distinctive wines, like their **barrel-fermented** white wine and their rosés, made not just from Bobal but also Cabernet Sauvignon, and which are reminiscent of the famous and beautifully-scented French rosés from Anjou. The rest of the range – **crianzas**, **reservas** and **gran reserva**s – are good wines, but not as distinctive as their special Bobals, **barrel-fermented** white wines and rosés. Pedro Navarro is so committed to his "**comarca**" (Utiel-Requena), like the Jacobite Viscount Stormont who was loyal only to the House of Stuart and to claret, and would rather be under the rule of Bordeaux than of England (for the claret, of course), showing how at that time wine, monarch and country were all of a piece.

It must be that loyalty to the Bobal grape and to Utiel-Requena that makes Pedro Navarro such a master of Bobal wines. He is also a master winemaker, who has taught generations of winemakers who go on in turn to make great wines in their own bodegas. I have always preferred educational advancement to the accident of birth. The former inspires confidence in professional abilities, the latter is no guarantee of quality.

Pedro has made a **barrel-fermented** old vine Bobal red in which the wood creeps up on you rather than jumping out. This **Coto d'Arcis** immediately displays its maker's qualities and background, beginning with its colour. It is a bright red, with flashes of garnet, whereas one might expect a more subdued, less brilliant red from old Bobal vines, but I have much to learn, and my own barrel-ageing continues. This **Coto d'Arcis** is in the line of those legendary New French Clarets from the Bordeaux of the Plantagenets, still made in some "lieu-dits" (a French term that refers to a specific vineyard that does not have a Premier or Grand Cru appellation), in the Médoc, Graves and Côtes de Bourg, in the heart of

Aquitaine.

Coto d'Arcis is a wine for drinking now, and it is also a summer red, despite being a mature wine. It does not need to be drunk with a meal or any particular food, but can and should be enjoyed on its own, or perhaps with one of Requena's famous "popular" sandwiches (fried ham, fried potato and a fried egg – a sort of English breakfast in a bun). **Sebirán** is one of those bodegas that has three or four outstanding wines, like this "madurado" red, made in good faith for its loyal devotees, just as Pedro Navarro is loyal to Utiel-Requena and to good Claret, and Viscount Stormont was to those same Clarets and the Stuarts. As Raimon Llull said, the paths of loyalty always run straight.[1]

Website: www.bodegasebiran.com
Label: Coto d'Arcis 2004
Type: Tinto madurado
ABV: 13.5%
Grape: Bobal
Approx. price: €3–4
Bodega: Sebirán
Address: C. Perez Galdós, 1, Campo Arcís, 46352 Requena, Valencia
Tel: 962301326
Fax: 962303966
Email: sebiran@tdv.net

NOTES

[1] Raimon Llull (or Lull) (1232–1315) was a mystic and poet born in Mallorca, whose writings widely influenced Neoplatonic mysticism throughout medieval Europe. Llull used logic and complex mechanical techniques (the "Ars magna") to relate all forms of knowledge, including theology, philosophy, and the natural sciences as analogues of one another and as manifestations of god in the universe.

Cum Laude:
Wine from the Source
Dominio Los Pinos, Fontanars (DO Valencia)

Fontanars is an organic outpost where nature, countryside and the spring waters are still so unspoilt that it stands to reason that Valencia's first organic bodega, **Los Pinos**, should be established here. The owner, Manuel Olaechea (see page 78), is a Peruvian agriculturalist who, convinced of the need for organic farming, sought out an ideal spot in which to establish his bodega. Of all the places he visited in Spain, France and Portugal, it was Fontanars that won his heart. Olaechea was a pioneer of organic farming in Peru, and he is committed to organic principles. His struggle reminds me of an anonymous twelfth-century Irish poem which warned, "Bad things are coming/few acorns, feeble forests and bad flowers/many cattle but scant milk/thin swine and hotheaded chieftains."

Advised by Professor Pertrucci of Fresno University in California (a world expert on wine-growing), he planted Cabernet Sauvignon, Cabernet Franc, Merlot, Sauvignon Blanc, Chardonnay and recently the wonderful Viognier from the Côtes du Rhône, which makes whites with an aroma of apricots and carnations, as well as Muscat Blanc à Petits Grains, which makes the magnificent Moscatels in those small appellations contrôlées in French Catalonia and Provence, though it will not be easy to grow here – Moscatel needs the sea, and the Mediterranean is some way off. **Cum Laude** is an organic blend of Monastrell, Syrah, Merlot and Cabernet Sauvignon. The result, how could it be otherwise, is a highly aromatic red with, as is often the case with organic wine, a sense of freshness and a natural vegetable earthiness. It has spent 12 months in French and American oak barrels, but here this element is less influential than the impact of the terroir, the grape varieties and, of course, the organic process. This **Cum Laude** is ready for drinking, it is from the 2002 harvest and is at its peak. Olaechea has not filtered the wine, and it may throw a natural sediment. This is all very natural and there are more and more wines of this type. It is easy to see why bodegas and winemakers are doing this, as the wine has a better aroma, but it is also a treat for the eyes. Everything about this wine gives pleasure, its commitment to being a natural product, its genuine reflection of the land and grapes it comes from and its generous bouquet. Organic farming is the last frontier for the defence of the character of our food, under onslaught from an increasingly artificial industry, with ever more processed food. This is neither gastronomy nor sustenance, given that it undermines our health and our very lives. Concentrating our poultry industry in three companies instead of having a range of local producers under the authority of a **"denominación de origen"**, or an organic authority, is a real and present danger to the population. Only true democracy (the government of the people, by the people, for the people, and not government by lobby), and a culture which prizes the enjoyment of food and where it comes from, will save us from disaster.

Website: None
Label: Cum Laude 2002
Type: tinto crianza ecológico
ABV: 13%
Grapes: Cabernet Sauvignon, Monastrell, Syrah, Merlot
Approx. price: €9–11
Bodega: Dominio Los Pinos
Address: Casa Los Pinos s/n, 46635 Fontanars dels Alforins, Valencia
Tel: 962222090
Fax: 96222208
Email: domlospinos@telefonica.net

Dagón:
The Essence of Bobal
Bodegas Dagón, Los Marcos (DO Utiel-Requena)

José Peñín[1] gave name to a new type of winemaker when he dubbed Pingus, from Ribera del Duero, a "vino de garaje" (garage wine). Small traditional bodegas had previously only differed from larger ones in volume of production, but their production methods were broadly similar. In contrast, the microbodegas that the brilliant seeker out of wines described as "garage", were something else again. I imagine that the garage connection refers to Apple or Microsoft (I always get confused, the computing dynasties have the same effect on me as our schoolroom lists of ancient kings) starting life in a garage. Naturally, Peñín wanted to emphasize that in a small, unprepossessing space you can make one of the great wines of the world, and the really important thing is know-how, culture, intelligence, rather than size. Of the four fundamental factors (soil, climate, vines and method) the vines and the method are crucial in these wines. Grape production is low, usually 300 to 400 grams per vine, which concentrates all the colour, aroma and flavour in the few grapes that the vine produces. Naturally, this requires a precision in the treatment of the vines that we might more readily associate with the exotic refinement of a bonsai garden. The method is based on grape selection – not merely the best, but only those that are perfect – chosen one by one. That is why these wines are expensive, as around 2.5 kilos of grapes are needed for each standard-sized bottle.

In Utiel-Requena they also make a garage wine, in Los Marcos. There you will find old Bobal vines from which Miguel Márquez makes 5,000 bottles of **Dagón** in his house-bodega. It is a mature red, full in the mouth, with intense and refined sweet tannins beautifully intertwined with the oak tannins. **Dagón** is the name of a Phoenician god – half man, half fish – equivalent to the Greek Dionysus. Miguel practises natural and biological agriculture, lovingly tending every vine on his four **hectares**. He harvests and selects only the best individual grapes, which he vinifies by means of lengthy **maceration** (there is no "remontage" – the process of circulating the liquid in the tank during fermentation) then ferments in French and American oak barrels, right through until springtime. Such slowness and attention to detail produce a lively wine, fine and radiant in its elegant maturity. Isn't elegance itself a product of maturity and absence of haste? **Dagón** is a red which undergoes lengthy ageing in wood, transferred to barrel in October 2002 for fermentation, and aged further in barrel until September 2004, when it was bottled. It spent all this time on its lees, but Miguel does not practise "bâtonnage" (basically stirring with a stick), he has confidence in what he knows and in the bountiful nature of Bobal from old vines, which are as dense and full of fruit as wild berries. This is Bobal in its pure state. Miguel is the embodiment of the old country saying, "de la vinya que be es conduix el llaurador instruit, trau profi" ("a vine well tended by growers who know, will see profit grow").

Website: www.dagon.es
Label: Dagón 2002 tinto
Type: tinto gran reserva
ABV: 15%
Grape: Bobal
Approx. price: €270
Bodega: Dagón
Address: Calle de la Cooperativa, 4, 46310 Los Marcos, Venta del Moro, Valencia
Tel/Fax: 962178056 652 667 521.
Email: dagonsad@yahoo.es.

NOTES

[1] José Peñín is Spain's equivalent to Robert Parker and produces the influential *Guía Peñín* every year, now also published annually in English as the *Peñín Guide to Spanish Wine*.

Daniel Belda Verdil:
Recovering Our Heritage
Bodegas Daniel Belda, Fontanars (DO Valencia)

Fontanars dels Alforins is an important winegrowing enclave, the richness of its soil and climate have meant it has always been one of the richest spots in the País Valenciano. From the creation of the kingdom of Valencia in the thirteenth century, the pattern of landownership here was closer to the Penedès in Catalonia than to l'Horta of Valencia due to the traditions of inheritance and homesteads, unlike the smallholdings of the coastal plain. This is a land blessed by nature, and its people have nurtured it. It stands 700 metres above sea level on average, and has a beautiful landscape in which the woods creep down towards the fields. Whatever was planted, be it vines, wheat or olives, the harvests were always plentiful, helped by water from natural springs and the high water table. The winegrowing tradition goes back a long time, and the local grape varieties, Verdil, Plantanova, Malvasia, Monastrell, **Garnacha Tintorera** and the rare Mandó, have been joined by interlopers (Tempranillo, Cabernet Sauvignon, Pinot Noir, Merlot and Chardonnay) that have taken well to this environment. These natural conditions have underpinned the success of the wines from Fontanars in the last fifteen years, but the quality of the land speaks volumes about those who work it. One of these, Daniel Belda, winemaker and owner of the eponymous bodega, is a key figure in the recent development of these wines, as he was one of the pioneers when he worked at **Dominio Los Pinos** (see pages 30 and 78) and he is also involved with the excellent wines from **Heretat de Taverners** nearby (see page 64).

In his own bodega he makes a **Cabernet Sauvignon Gran Reserva** and a **Merlot Reserva**, the former being longer-lasting and earthier, while the latter is fuller and smoother, subtle and seductive, as is the **Selección Reserva**, which combines the two. The **barrel-fermented Belda Pinot Noir** is an intriguing wine, whose aromas of ripe forest berries, alongside elegant tannins from the barrel, give it a sensual quality. It is a bit like a Burgundy, but is also reminiscent of South African Pinotage, a new hybrid of Pinot Noir and Cinsault. Daniel has another great winemaking distinction – he was behind the recovery of the local Verdil white grape, the traditional grape in the Clariano **subzone** (La Costera and the Vall d'Albaida). This grape was generally sold in bulk so that its qualities could be harnessed to other wines not similarly blessed. It was not thought of as a grape capable of making quality modern white wines. Daniel showed that this was far from being the case when he made his fruity wine, all apples and pears, but also boasting a good structural backbone. This grape oxidizes very quickly, and you have to be a very good winemaker (which Daniel is) not to lose its sharp freshness in the process of fermentation. If it is ripe, the grape emphasizes certain qualities (alcohol, colour, fullness), if it is a touch too young, it is green, acid and lacking in fruit. Belda has achieved an excellent balance of the qualities of this capricious but rewarding grape in his own **Daniel Belda Verdil**. More than that, he has opened the door for further work on this grape. There is still a magnificent Verdil waiting in the wings. Juan Carlos Gabils, one of the best chefs in the country and a teacher at the Valencia Restaurant School, has created a dish using this wine, and as the Eleventh Winemaking Commandment says, thou shalt not be a great wine until thou art used in a great dish. It is true that vines and people are alike, as is shown by this wine that seemed to be one thing but turns out to be another. As Alphonse Karr (1808-1890) said, "Every man has three characters: the one he has, the one he shows, and the one he thinks he has."

Website: www.danielbelda.com
Label: Daniel Belda Verdil
Type: Blanco joven
ABV: 13%
Grape: Verdil
Approx. price: €3–4
Bodega: J. Belda
Address: Avda. Conde Salvatierra 54, 46635 Fontanars dels Alforins, Valencia
Tel: 962222278
Fax: 962222245
Email: info@danielbelda.com

Dominio de la Vega Especial:
A Singular Cava
Dominio de la Vega, San Antonio (DO Utiel-Requena)

Dominio de la Vega is a Cava created only a few years ago by Fermín Pardo, Emilio Expósito and Álvaro Faubel, who were among the original shareholders of Torre Oria Wines and Cava, but they left after internal business disagreements. These three musketeers, with their magnificent fighting spirit, started all over again by setting up another bodega to make quality wines and Cavas. And they've done it. The range of wines is excellent, especially the **Añacal** oak-aged white (Macabeo) and red (Bobal, Tempranillo and Cabernet Sauvignon). They also make two Cavas: **Brut** and **Brut Reserva**. The former is young, dry, very fruity with small and neat bubbles. The other is a unique and remarkable Cava. The annual Enoforum wine fair voted it Spain's best in 2004 and again in 2006 (the result of a blind tasting by winemakers from different Spanish bodegas). The **Brut Reserva** is seductive, with its small, fine bubbles, rising up the glass like a well-drilled infantry regiment, with long-lasting effervescence. It has good fruit, but also shows that hint of age which **reserva** Cavas achieve after resting with the yeast lees in the bottleneck after clarification.

We have before us a great Cava, clean, natural and aromatic, with hints of nut (walnut and hazelnut) and very much a Brut with just five grams of sugar per litre. A good Cava depends on the quality of the final "shipping dosage" (usually sugar plus some of the same wine that has been reserved for this purpose) added immediately before final bottling. I have seen fine Cavas ruined by the addition of dosages from hell. The **Dominio de la Vega** shipping dosage is exceptional, clean, honest and healthy. All of these qualities are characteristic of the winemaker, Daniel Expósito, who after studying at the Requena Wine School spent time at König Rheingau in Germany. The German sparkling wine industry is the most advanced when it comes to secondary fermentation, and though they have generally gone for second fermentation in tank (the Charmat Method) rather than in bottle, their use of technology and their winemaking culture is masterly. I have had the honour of being on the tasting committee of the leading Sekt producer, Henkell in Wiesbaden, and few professional experiences have been as educational.

Dominio de la Vega is based in a restored eighteenth-century building that is well worth a visit, and which has its own story as an exiled count's residence that eventually became a wine mansion. And this is exactly what this bodega is, a mansion of Cavas and fine wines.

Website: www.dominiodelavega.com
Label: Dominio de la Vega especial
Type: Brut reserva 24 months in cellar
ABV: 12%
Grapes: Macabeo, Chardonnay
Approx. price: €17–18
Bodega: Dominio de la Vega
Address: Carretera Madrid-Valencia km 270, San Antonio 46340, Valencia
Tel: 962320570
Fax: 962320330
Email: info@dominiodelavega.com

Dominio de la Vega:
Mastering Oak
Dominio de la Vega, San Antonio (DO Utiel-Requena)

Happily, tastes in wine change; we are not drinking the same wines that we drank twenty years ago. This change has given rise to a transformation as great as the one that took place in the last third of the nineteenth century, and it has been more cultural than technological. It has seen the emergence of a style of red wine that is halfway between an unoaked "joven" and an oak-aged "**crianza**", and which has been given various names: "madurado" (matured), "semicrianza" (semicrianza), "roble" (oaked), "4 meses en barrica" (4 months in barrel). These all mean that the wine has spent no more than four or five months in barrel and that it combines the freshness and fruit of a young wine with the light oxidation and touch of wood afforded by a short period of ageing. Of all the names tried, the best appears to be sticking in **DO** Utiel-Requena: "madurado". "Semicrianza" sounds half-baked; 4 months in barrel has a touch of coitus interruptus, and oaked sounds like furniture. "Madurado", on the other hand, conveys that it is not a **crianza** that is being aimed at, but a new, different style. The idea emerged in the 1990s within the most demanding client in the wine-buying world: the Sunday Times Wine Club. Those first "matured" wines opened the way for aromatic reds that emphasized ripe fruit, spiced up with a few months effective ageing, but soft enough to drink on their own. In 1995 The Sunday Times Wines Club offered a selection of "matured winter reds", that was a massive success. That remarkable mixed dozen contained a sunny Californian Eagle Falls, the ample Château de Calce from the Côtes de Roussillon, a great Clos de Château de Beaune from Burgundy, the remarkable Domaine des Hortensias and a magnificent wine from Utiel-Requena, Villa Albosa.

As Hugh Johnson, the club president, said in his Christmas greeting to members that year, these wines were "a revelation, exciting and good regional innovation". The author worked closely with the club's tasters and buyers in Reading (where Oscar Wilde wrote his "Ballad of Reading Gaol"), and it was a wonderful experience and apprenticeship.

The success of the "madurados" from Utiel-Requena has been great news for Valencian wine. The different wines of this type sell a million bottles a year. The consumer appreciates the qualities of these generous and harmonious wines that are full of subtlety and complexity.

One of the best is **Dominio de la Vega** 2003, made from Bobal, Tempranillo and Cabernet Sauvignon (in equal proportions), of which 35,000 bottles were produced. The main characteristic of these "madurados" is their enticing allure, and as Oscar Wilde observed, everything can be resisted except temptation. **Domino de la Vega** underwent malolactic fermentation in barrel and this gives it a touch of buttered toast. The barrels were both new and used, as these wines should not be overdone with the wood of the new barrels. The wine has an intriguingly subdued cherry colour with violet overtones, and combines smells of forest fruit with highland herbs.

Website: www.dominiodelavega.com
Label: Dominio de la Vega 2004
Type: Madurado tinto
ABV: 13%
Grapes: Bobal, Tempranillo, Cabernet Sauvignon
Approx. price: €5
Bodega: Dominio de la Vega
Dirección: Ctra. Madrid-Valencia, km. 270,6. San Antonio. Requena 46390 (Valencia)
Teléfono: 962320570
Fax: 962320330
Email: info@dominiodelavega.com

Domus Romans:
The Household Gods of Wine
Bodegas Valle del Carche, El Pinós (DO Alicante)

The Valle del Carche is a lovely "**comarca**" straddling the border between the **Comunidad Valenciana** and Murcia. The paranoid nineteenth-century redrawing of provincial boundaries saw part of the area allocated to Murcia, where it has stayed, so far, but the inhabitants have retained their language (Valencian), their culture, their gastronomy and their wines. As stated previously, Marx said that to know a country one must have eaten its bread and drunk its wine, and the Valle del Carche is as Valencian as La Safor or El Comtat. Its rices and stews (especially the paella of rabbit and snails finished off with a great final blast of flame when "aliagas" and "sarmientos" – gorse and vine shoots – are added to the wood fire right at the end) and its hearty, aromatic Monastrell wines, the like of which led Petronius to say "Vita vinum est" ("Wine is life").[1] The impressive Sierra del Carche mountains protect the "**comarca**" and the gently undulating plains bear a passing resemblance to the Cape winelands in South Africa, and so do the wines. The landscape is beautiful particularly the lower forest, with its pine trees and local oak encroaching into the olive groves and vineyards as if they were one and the same. In the midst of all this natural plenty stand the **Bodegas del Valle de Carche** with their "**fincas**" Bellavista, Alberquilla and Casa del Olmo, built with the rustic good taste that characterizes old Valencian farms and homesteads, which any editor of *House & Garden* magazine would swoon over.

This bodega makes various Monastrell wines, to modern tastes but without losing their own character. These include the ebullient **Porta Regia** (see page 96) and a **Fondillón** that is still being aged but will eventually emerge as a great wine. Additionally, Cabernet Sauvignon, Tempranillo, Syrah and Merlot are used to make blends that have a local feel, but are also part of winegrowing currents that are drawing together the southern hot-climate winegrowing world (South Africa, California, Australia), as explained by Professor Winkler of the UC Davis Department of Viticulture and Oenology in California.

The **Domus** range is in the classical mould. **Domus Romans Reserva** is made with Tempranillo, Cabernet Sauvignon and Merlot, and is an alluring brick red, light ochre colour with a velvety sheen that lights up the glass. It has a notable aroma of grilled peppers and soft, slightly tart tannins, that give the wine its freshness and smoothness. In the mouth it is round and velvety, with a certain balsamic vigour, the ideal accompaniment to the typical rice and tomato dishes of the area, like those served in Casa Ricardo in Raspay.[2] **Domus** spends fourteen months in French oak barrels from Alliers and fine-grained American oak from Missouri. The final time in oak is spent in older barrels. This goes against the wisdom of some wine gurus who insist on new oak barrels, but these can overwhelm the subtleties of the grape. Experienced bodegas like **Valle del Carche** prefer to use both. They are like the elegant and beautiful Eleanor Parker in the film "The Naked Jungle", in response to her husband (by proxy) Charlton Heston's complaints at her being a widow when he had to have everything brand new (the furniture, the piano, the wife); "If you knew anything about music, you'd know that the best piano is one that's been played." The beautiful array of barrels in **Valle del Carche**, both new and old, which store the **Domus** and the **Porta Regia** are like calm goddesses from on high watching over their world.

Website: www.valledelcarche.es
Label: Domus Romans
Type: Tinto Reserva
ABV: 13%
Grapes: Tempranillo, Cabernet Sauvignon
Approx. price: €12
Bodega: Valle del Carche
Address: Paseo de la Constitución, 76 A, 03650 Pinoso, Alicante
Tel: 965978349
Fax: 965978060
Email: info@valledelcarche

NOTES

[1] Petronius (*c.* 27–66) was the author of the bawdy *Satyricon* (the quote is from section 34), written for the enjoyment of the court of the emperor Nero.

[2] Restaurant Casa Ricardo is in the village of Raspay on the Murcia–Alicante border.

El Sequé:
The Triumph of Monastrell
Bodegas y Viñedos El Sequé, El Pinós (DO Alicante)

The slopes of the Sierra del Carche, west of El Pinós, have always produced good red wine. This is land where Monastrell works well, down the road from Monòver at the southern limit of the País Valenciano, producing thick, full-bodied, viscous reds with a fragrance that increases with time. The location is ideal for a project like this one, set up by Agapito Rico from Jumilla jointly with Bodegas Artadi from Rioja, with the aim of making an "**alta expresión**" Monastrell of indisputable excellence. This they have achieved.

Although Monastrell predominates, some Cabernet Sauvignon and Syrah have been added. **El Sequé** is a wine for laying down (it has spent twelve months in barrel) and will be at its best from 2007. The fragrance of ripe fruit: cassis and sweet cherry blended with a delicate aroma of blueberry and balsam, characteristic of Monastrell, and of Syrah, two eastern Mediterranean varietals that have several similarities, while Cabernet Sauvignon serves to slow down oxidation and provide that touch of astringency for sinew and vibrancy. The element of acidity provided by the Cabernet Sauvignon harmonizes well on the nose with the sweetness of the Monastrell and the Syrah, and it is all rounded off with full, sweet tannins.

El Sequé is made by **Bodegas y Viñedos El Sequé**, in the area of the same name, where they grow 40 **hectares** of Syrah, Cabernet Sauvignon and old vines of Monastrell. This is without doubt the best red from the Vinalopó, a treat to drink, the final confirmation of Monastrell's suitability for these "**vinos de alta expresión**", and of the grape's star quality. **El Sequé** are also planning to make a **Fondillón**, which would be a great joy, as I have spent much of my life beating the drum for this wine. I will observe attentively, and I hope that the people from **El Sequé** will be able to combine their modern technology and know-how with the wine culture required for an undertaking of this kind, something that is rarer than one might think among winemakers and winegrowers. The **El Sequé** enterprise might begin by mentioning in their catalogue the background to their Alicante wines and their **Fondillón**, because otherwise they will have read and used the core texts, but they will have omitted to pay their dues to those who paved the way, and their project, one of the finest that I have seen in many years, deserves to take its place righteously and by right.

Website: www.artadi.com
Label: El Sequé 2002
Type: Vino de guarda de crianza
ABV: 13.5%
Approx. price: €15–17
Grapes: Monastrell, Syrah, Cabernet Sauvignon
Bodega: Laderas del Pinoso
Address: El Sequé, 59, 03650 El Pinós, Alicante
Tel: 945600119
Fax: 945600850
Email: elseque@artadi.com

Emilio Clemente:
In the Clasp of the River Cabriel
Emilio Clemente, Finca Caballero (DO Utiel-Requena)

The Utiel-Requena **Denominación de Origen** is one of Europe's most important winegrowing areas, outstanding in both the quality and variety of its wines: reds, whites, rosés and Cavas. Utiel-Requena has better soil for wine than Ribera del Duero and a better climate than Rioja, and its reds have seen it become a notable **Denominación de Origen**. Its history of selling in bulk weighs heavily, but the new wines make friends wherever they go and bring prestige to the area, winning over both critics and public. This is the case with **Emilio Clemente**, a young bodega that makes wine from its vines in a beautiful spot surrounded by hills on the border of the Valencia region, by the meandering river Cabriel. There are 98 **hectares** of Cabernet Sauvignon, Tempranillo and Merlot. Grapegrowers since 1986, Emilio Clemente and María Carmen Luján decided to make wine rather than sell their grapes. Their bodega in Requena is made up of a series of magnificently restored buildings which are set to become a very beautiful expression of wine-related architecture, perfect for establishing a social, cultural and commercial project capable of making these wines a byword for class and glamour; since Emilio and María Carmen, a couple with class and intelligence, have created a very elegant red. The bodega incorporates the very latest technology, but they do not overlook the fact that the game is won in the vineyards down by the river Cabriel.

In the late 1970s, in an effort to develop a wine culture in Spain, Xavier Domingo, José Peñín and Miguel A. Torres wrote books – *El vino trago a trago* (Dédalo, 1980), *Manual de vinos españoles* (Pentathlon, 1981) and *Viñas y vinos* (Blume, 1978), respectively – that sparked the interest of beginners and reaffirmed the faith of the converted. In the latter work Miguel Torres tells the story, endlessly repeated since then, of his remark to some admiring visitors to the hi-tech Torres bodega, that a good wine is not made in there, but out in the vineyards. Emilio and María Carmen keep this in mind when making their **Emilio Clemente crianza** and the "madurado" **Peñas Negras**. The property has a microclimate that sees the wines ripen early as a result of the reflection of sunlight off the river and the surrounding hillsides, as in the Mosel and the Rhine. **Emilio Clemente crianza** is a red wine in the Bordeaux style. The Cabernet

Sauvignon has done its job well. It has a nose full of raspberry, vanilla, green pepper and butter, with a subtle presence of oak whispering in the ear and the heart of the drinker. This is a fine red wine which will be even better if kept for a time to mature. It is the same with wine as with people, the better you treat them, the better they treat you.

Website: None
Label: Emilio Clemente crianza 2001
Type: tinto crianza
ABV: 12.5%
Grapes: Cabernet Sauvignon, Tempranillo
Approx. price: €9–11
Bodega: Emilio Clemente
Address: Camino San Blas, s/n, 46340 Requena, Valencia
Tel: 963173584
Fax: 963173726
Email: info@eclemente.es

Estrecho:
A Modern Monastrell
Bodegas Mendoza, L'Alfàs del Pi (DO Alicante)

In October 2005 **Bodegas Enrique Mendoza** from the Alicante **Denominación de Origen** launched a lovingly nurtured project, **Estrecho**, their Monastrell monovarietal. Mendoza already make an excellent Monastrell, **Dolç de Mendoza**, an elegant and delicate dessert wine, made from fully ripe grapes. The great excitement surrounding any new wine brought out by **Bodegas Mendoza** is due to two factors. First, that this bodega has such a good track record and produces such well-defined and excellent wines that people are eagerly waiting for what comes next. Secondly, the confidence that the **Mendoza bodega** has earned through successfully planting, adapting and making wine from the most eminent grapes on the planet: Cabernet Sauvignon, Merlot, Syrah, Pinot Noir (their latest Cabernet and Syrah blend is a fantasy of aromas). This is the much-envied Mendoza recipe for making successful wines.

In a textbook from which many of us learnt the rudiments of our trade, *La vid y los vinos españoles* (Marsiega, 1942) by the Valencian Miguel Comenge (republished by his son, the owner of Bodegas Comenge in Ribera del Duero), the Monastrell grape is described as producing wines of an intense, deep colour. The first triumph of this red **Estrecho** is its colour. José ("Pep") Mendoza (see also page 104) has managed magisterially, as usual, to make a red Monastrell which retains the grape's virtues but without overdoing the colour, which is very important in coping with the tendency of this grape to oxidize, as in dry, hot zones, more colour means more oxidizing enzymes are present during the development of the wine. **Estrecho** is a remarkable wine, the very model of a modern Monastrell, elegant, delicate and complex, with a clean, smooth taste, and a successful balance of the two factors that are hard to harmonize in a southern red, fresh fruit: figs, cherries, plums, alongside spice (vanilla and cinnamon). **Estrecho** spends fourteen months in 500 litre casks of French oak, one of the good decisions that go into achieving the great quality of this wine, as barrels of this quality lend a more subtle oak presence to the wine, as well as allowing less microoxigenation with the consequent reduction in the grape's tendency to oxidize.

Pep Mendoza has made another great wine thanks to his skills as a winemaker, acquired during his stints overseas (New Zealand, California,

Chile), and his eagerness to rethink the winemaking he was first taught. **Bodegas Mendoza** also has on its property in Villena one of the most modern and hi-tech wine operations in all of Spain. A state-of-the-art system for measuring the underground humidity of the vine and its nutrients, and a system of protecting panels that open out automatically when the sun is at its fiercest so that the stoma (openings through which the solar energy is transformed into colours, aromas and flavours) of the vineleaves stay open. This modern viticulture is the basis of the quality of the wines **Bodegas Enrique Mendoza**. Pep thinks of himself as a grower of grapes and sees each vine as the source of the qualities he is aiming for.

Website: www.bodegasmendoza.com
Label: Estrecho 2000
Type: tinto crianza
ABV: 14%
Grape: Monastrell
Approx. price: €18–20
Bodega: Enrique Mendoza
Address: Partida El Romeral s/n, 03580 L'Alfás del Pi, Alicante
Tel/Fax: 965888639
Email: bodegas-mendoza@bodegasmendoza.com

Fernando Francés Chardonnay:
A Natural Wine
Fernando Francés, Moixent (DO Valencia)

Els Corrals is an organic estate 600 metres above sea level on the main road between Moixent and Fontanars, in a beautiful spot on the way up to the Fontanars high plateau, and it is where **Bodegas Fernando Francés** make their organic wines. Moixent is recovering its winemaking heritage. Nearby stands the hilltop Iberian settlement of La Bastida de les Alcusses dating from the fourth century BC, which is well worth a visit. Here archaeological finds have revealed the importance of wine for the Iberians and their winemaking methods. **Bodegas Fernando Francés** have restored an eighteenth-century wine trough which is itself worth seeing. The **finca** cultivates 50 **hectares** of Cabernet Sauvignon, Tempranillo, Merlot and Chardonnay vines, grown according to organic methods. **Fernando Francés** has chosen the organic option in order to make natural wine. The red wines include **Viña Soler crianza** made with Cabernet Sauvignon, Tempranillo and Merlot, as well as single variety wines under the label **Fernando Francés**.

Organic wines, in addition to the qualities asociated with their natural production, contain the spirit of civic solidarity that inspires those who make it. Organic ideas are taking root, but we are still a long way from respecting and living in harmony with the environment. This bodega exports to Germany, Switzerland and Scandinavia, whose citizens are generally more advanced in these matters. Here, even among some environmentalists we find the pernicious NIMBY (Not In My Back Yard) syndrome – for instance, wind is the cleanest and most sustainable source of energy, but no one wants a wind farm in their "**comarca**". We must recover our collective civic solidarity, and a good place to start is by drinking this **barrel-fermented** Chardonnay made by **Fernando Francés**. This is a classic Chardonnay that is harvested fully ripe, and fermented in French oak barrels. Chardonnay and French oak is a marriage made in heaven, adding nuttiness (hazelnut and walnut) as well as hints of apple and pear to the grape's typical pineapple flavours. There is some pistachio alongside a green and grassy clean, natural taste characteristic of organic wines. It has a wonderful bouquet, which as the great Frona Eunice Wait Colburn said, is the soul of a wine.[1] Fernando Francés's Chardonnay is a wine with soul, at one with the spirit of nature in a way that is largely forgotten, but thankfully not by everyone; there are still a few people out there with the environmental awareness needed to undertake something like this.

Web: www.eco-wine.net
Label: Chardonnay 2002
Type: barrel-fermented white
ABV: 12.5%
Grape: Chardonnay
Approx. price: €7–9
Bodega: Fernando Francés
Address: Ctra. Moixent-Fontanars km. 11, 46640 Moixent, Valencia
Tel: 962132315
Fax: 963852326
Email: eco-wine@ono.com

NOTES

[1] Frona Eunice Wait Colburn (1859—*c.* 1946) was a Californian journalist and writer. Her books include *Wines & Vines of California; or, A Treatise on the Ethics of Wine Drinking* (1889; repr. Howell-North Books, 1973) and the novel *In Old Vintage Days* (John Henry Nash, 1937). She was the butt of Ambrose Bierce's humour in his poem "The Competitor" (1909) for her involvement in women's issues. It begins:

> Mrs Frona Eunice Wait,
> My legs are not so very straight;
> My spine, I'm sorry to observe
> Maintains a most rebellious curve

Finca Terrerazo:
Wine from the Land

Bodegas Mustiguillo (Vino de la Tierra El Terrerazo)[1]

Antonio Sarrión, the creator of the celebrated **Finca Terrerazo** and **Quincha Corral** red wines, also makes a different wine altogether, **Mestizaje** (see page 84), that is superior to the first two. Discerning wine drinkers rave about the superior definition and refinement of **Mestizaje**. The higher price of the other two is irrelevant, as price is a matter of supply and demand that is not always reflected in higher quality. Good quality is no longer an attribute as it was a couple of decades ago, now it is a requirement of the market and quality control.

Readers of this collection devoted to the wines of the **Comunidad Valenciana** will have noted that I consider all of these to be quality wines, as otherwise they would neither be in the marketplace nor under the aegis of the various official bodies that protect the product and the consumer: "**Denominación de Origen**", "Vino de la Tierra", "Indicación Geográfica Protegida". All of this derives from EU legislation relating to "Quality Wine Expression" according to the legislation of the member state. Quality here is a descriptive term rather than a categorical one. If on occasion a wine is described as "gran calidad" this is generally due to specific additional legal requirements relating to organic wines, **reservas**, dessert wines, "crus" or "vins de garde". The qualification excellent used to be reserved for wines that had earned the term for their outstanding quality and definition.

As Sarrión rightly says, "the task of the winemaker is to produce a wine to be enjoyed from the moment that it goes on sale." I could not agree more, though this is truer of his 2003 **Finca Terrerazo** than of previous vintages, and it was this aspect that the connoisseurs were identifying and which was enticing them towards the **Mestizaje** rather than the more heavyweight **Terrerazo** and **Quincha Corral**. None of us should fall into the trap of distinguishing between wines for tasting and wines for drinking. All wines are for drinking, and all wines should be tasted, as this serves to introduce the wine to our different senses. If we taste a wine and it is not ready for drinking, that means it is not good, which is why we try it before pouring out a full glass. That is why I agree wholeheartedly with Antonio Sarrión, and why I am so gratified that

Finca Terrerazo has come back to the real world. This 2003 **Terrerazo** is far superior to its predecessors, and is truer to the style of a true Bobal (65%) wine even with the presence alongside of cooler climate varieties like Cabernet Sauvignon and Tempranillo. It has spent twenty months in new Alliers oak casks, and **maceration** and fermentation took place in magnificent French oak containers. Sarrión has produced 30,000 bottles of this fine **Terrerazo**. It will have a long life, the maturity of its bouquet deriving from the age of the Bobal vines. It is a pure vermilion colour with a touch of viscosity. The nose (a mingling of the aromas and the taste) is refined and elegant, lightly spiced with an intriguing hint of toast. I very much like the touch of truffle in the aftertaste and the overall harmony and balance. It is a Mediterranean red with the personality of the wine territory to which **Bodegas Mustiguillo** belongs (its very own Vinos de la Tierra el Terrarazo rather than Utiel-Requena). But this wine is made with the leading Utiel-Requena grape and in the same climate and soil. Manuel Vázquez Montalbán's great detective Pepe Carvalho used to tell the story of a hard-nosed and pragmatic CIA agent of his acquaintance, who liked to say, "If it looks like a duck, walks like a duck and has feathers like a duck, maybe it is a duck."[2]

Website: None
Label: Finca Terrerazo 2003
Type: Tinto de reserva de finca
ABV: 14.5%
Grapes: Bobal, Cabernet Sauvignon, Tempranillo
Approx. price: €20–23
Bodega: Mustiguillo
Address: Ctra. N-330 km 195, 46300 El Terrerazo, Las Cuevas de Utiel, Valencia
Tel: 962304575
Fax: 962301964
Email: mustiguillo@inicia.es

NOTES

[1] Finca Terrerazo have opted to remain outside the **Denominación de Origen** system, and have achieved their own nomenclature as a Vino de la Tierra.

[2] The late Manuel Vázquez Montalbán (1939–2003) is much missed as a writer, cultural and political commentator, broadcaster and gourmet.

Fondillón Salvador Poveda:
In the Name of the Father
Salvador Poveda, Monòver (DO Alicante)

Salvador Poveda Luz (Monòver 1926–Alicante 1981) was one of the finest wine men that this country has produced. Trained as a wine-maker in Requena, he was part of a generation which, under the guidance of "maestre" Pascual Carrión (director of the Requena Wine School from 1941–61), began the process of recovery of Valencian wine. Salvador Poveda modernized the wines of Alicante, making genuine Monastrell rosés, aromatic young reds, and a **crianza** red that was absolutely unique, his much missed Doble Capa. But where he really showed his mastery was in the recovery of the mythical **Fondillón** de Alicante, which from the fifteenth to the nineteenth centuries was Europe's most noble and elegant wine. By the mid-fifteenth century the Alicante "**huerta**" had become a leading wine centre on the back of its Monastrell, brought from Greece 200 years previously by the Almogavars (see page 10). These vigorous vines produced powerful, aromatic red wines, high in colour, strength, residual sugar and acidity.

Soon wineries throughout Europe were sending their agents to Alicante. A German traveller, Heteronymous Münzer, has left us an account of this traffic in his diary of 1494, "...from the town of Alicante a great quantity of exquisite wine is obtained..."[1] Stored in barrels, which were also used to transport it, Alicante's red wine continued to age and improve; the name **Fondillón** suggests that it was in the bottom ("fondo") of the barrel that this transformation took place. It was soon sent on long ocean journeys, on which its qualities were highly prized. Over the succeeding centuries **Fondillón** remained a wine of great pres-tige on Europe's tables, and in its literature. In *The Count of Montecristo*, the hero shares some **Fondillón** and biscuits with Cavalcanti ("Now," said the count, "what will you take – a glass of port, sherry, or Alicante?" "Alicante, if you please; it is my favourite wine").

Fondillón disappeared during the upheavals produced in Europe's wines by the phylloxera parasite in the nineteenth century, until Salvador Poveda rescued it from oblivion, and in 1976 he brought out the first bot-tle, from the 1959 harvest. **Fondillón** is a noble dessert wine, Alicante's vintage wine, transformed by time into a delicious nectar full of spices, mature tobacco, poached fruit and toasted wood. The taste is dry, but with a residue of sweetness, honeyed and with a touch of liquorice. Its production is limited, being made only in good years, and then only a few thousand bottles' worth. **Fondillón** confirms Cicero's remark on the effect of ageing on men and wine.[2]

Website: www.salvadorpoveda.com
Label: Fondillón Salvador Poveda 1980
Type: Fondillón de Alicante
ABV: 15%
Grape: Monastrell
Age: 15 years in barrel
Approx. price: €23–25
Bodega: Salvador Poveda
Address: Benjamin Palencia 19, 03640 Monòver, Alicante
Tel: 966960180
Fax: 965473389
Email: salvadorpoveda@salvadorpoveda.com

NOTES

[1] Jerónimo Münzer, *Viaje por España y Portugal (1494–95)* (Ediciones Polifemo, 1991). Münzer was a physician and geographer from Nuremberg who fled plague in his city at this time to travel around the Iberian peninsula. In these writings he provides a wealth of detail about daily life in Spain at the end of the fifteenth century.

[2] Marcus Tullius Cicero, *De senectute* (On Old Age), "Sic se res habet: ut enim non omne vinum, sic non omnis natura vetustate coacescit" (The fact is that, just as it is not every wine, so it is not every life that turns sour from keeping).

Fusta Nova:
Moscatel from the Forest
Bodega Vicente Gandia, Chiva (DO Valencia)

Fusta Nova is a sweet wine made with Moscatel of Alexandria by **Bodegas Gandia**. This company is one of the largest exporters of bottled Spanish wine. It was founded in 1885 by a Valencian, Vicente Gandia, and nowadays is an international company run by José María Gandia, the founder's grandson. They have bodegas in Utiel-Requena (the Hoya de Cadenas property in Las Cuevas) and Valencia (Chiva). They produce, in addition to millions of bottles of branded wine, a range of quality wines (the reds **Ceremonia** and **Generación 1** – see page 56) and, best of all, **Fusta Nova**, an excellent "**vin doux naturel**".

Though there are divergent opinions as to the bodega's overall style and its use of its position in the market, it is undeniable that this is one of the most professional winemaking outfits in Spain. To sell millions of bottles year after year in such difficult and demanding markets as the UK, the wines must be free of any weaknesses, and to achieve this you need to run a tight ship, which **Bodegas Gandia** does. It is true to say that for the consumer it can be confusing to navigate the different styles, a common characteristic of bodegas that are both high volume brand producers and have a range of quality wines. But the truth is that we have before us a great wine: **Fusta Nova** ("New Wood" in Valencian). Everything about this wine suggests intelligence and good taste, from the initial concept to its development, not forgetting its Valencian name (a masterstroke that associates the product uniquely with its birthplace and makes it difficult for similar wines to challenge it).

Fusta Nova is made with grapes carefully selected from old vines. The "mosto flor" (free run juice flowing from grapes crushed by their own weight without any mechanical pressing) is cold fermented with the grape skins at 15–16°C – this skin maceration is carried out to get the freshest and most intense fruit flavours (Moscatel, pear and quince). The Moscatel grape, as **Gandia** have shown, can then be enhanced further with time in barrels of new French Alliers oak, from where it gets that full, silky taste, with a hint of toasted wood and walnut. Alliers oak adds these subtleties to the Moscatel, typical of fine-grained oak from the forests of France's Massif Central, and the three months it spends in barrel are just right, since aromatic varieties like Moscatel are quick to oxidize, noticeable above all in the colour. **Fusta Nova** has a limpid brilliance, it needs to be drunk cool, and goes as well with foie gras at the start of a meal as it does with cheesecake at the end.

Website: www.vicentegandia.com
Label: Fusta Nova
Type: sweet wine
ABV: 15%
Grape: Moscatel de Alejandría
Approx. Price: €7–8 (50 cl)
Bodega: Vicente Gandia
Address: Ctra. Cheste-Godelleta, s/n, 46370 Chiva, Valencia
Tel: 962524242
Fax: 962524243
Email: info@vicentegandia.com

Generación 1:
Ready for Trade
Bodega Vicente Gandia (DO Utiel-Requena)

For a company to last over a hundred years is quite an achievement and no easy feat, so for a Valencian bodega to reach the ripe old age of 120 is a good thing, which goes to show both the vigour of the wine sector and the quality of its wines. An eminent Californian wine-maker, Francis Ford Coppola, has said that no industry that makes a bad product survives. 120 years encompasses four generations. For this to happen takes a lot of work and and a lot of getting things right. Of course, **Bodegas Gandia** possesses state-of-the-art technology and kit, but the most important elements behind the company's longevity are the hearts and minds of all those involved. As Javier Gandia, a member of the fourth generation, points out, it takes a lot of man-hours to ensure the highest quality product and highest levels of customer satisfaction.

To celebrate the latest milestone, **Bodegas Gandia** has produced just 24,000 bottles of a limited edition wine, **Generación 1**, in honour of the founder, Vicente Gandia. It is a 13% ABV red wine made with seventy percent Bobal from mature vines alongside thirty percent Cabernet Sauvignon and Garnacha from their Hoya de Cadenas estate. In this wine domaine the closeness of the grapes to the winery is guaranteed, as is the quality control, something to which Gandia brings an almost Teutonic thoroughness. It could not be otherwise, because selling in over 80 countries around the world, some of them as demanding as Britain and as vast as the USA, requires the top-notch professionalism and entrepreneurial brio of someone like José María Gandia – the third and presiding generation. **Generación 1** conveys all the skill and verve of this wine family. It could be described as a "**tinto de alta expresión**" given the intensity of the aromas – the **maceration** with the grapeskins lasts twenty days. This is doubly praiseworthy bearing in mind the difficulty of ageing Bobal in barrel. The wine spends twelve months in barrels of new French (Alliers) and American (Missouri) oak. A good combination and a statement of winemaking know-how, as the conductibility of the Bobal is tricky when it comes to barrel ageing. The result is, of course, a fine wine, whose first notes are an elegant underlying aroma (the result of the medium toasting of the good wood in which it is aged), combined harmoniously with aromas of ripe plum and a touch of cassis, alongside – as you would expect from a blend of the three such distinctive grape varieties – an array of plant and floral scents (holly and geranium) which achieve an overall balance – nothing rough or prickly. Its palate is slightly spicy, with the characteristic pepper (toasted here) of Cabernet Sauvignon being underpinned by the inevitable, omnipresent and foreseeable presence of liquorice, characteristic of the "grands crus". This makes decanting the wine a pleasure as well as an obligation. **Generación 1** is a red wine that will last a long time, and at each stage of its development its bouquet will move up a notch, adding to the pleasure to be had in following its progress. Walt Whitman wrote in "Song of Myself" in *Leaves of Grass*: "…bound my own way ready for trade, my joints the limberest joints on earth and the sternest joints on earth,"[1] as those of the Gandia clan must have been for them to last and trade for so long.

Website: www.vicentegandia.com
Label: Generación 1 2003
Type: Tinto vino de guarda
ABV: 13%
Grapes: Bobal, Cabernet Sauvignon, Garnacha
Approx. price: €25
Bodega: Vicente Gandia
Address: Ctra. Cheste-Godelleta s/n, 46370 Chiva, Valencia
Tel: 962524242
Fax: 962524243
Email: info@vicentegandia.com

NOTES

[1] Walt Whitman, *Leaves of Grass* (first published 1855), "Song of Myself", section 16.

Gracel Bobal:
Mature Splendour
Bodega Enotec, Requena (DO Utiel-Requena)

Rafael Ochando, winemaker at good old Vinícola Requenense, is also a teacher at the Requena Wine School alongside Félix Cuartero, and a firm defender of his beloved Requena. Both have fought, professionally and personally, on behalf of the region's viticulture and, especially, on behalf of the Bobal grape. This Iberian varietal, more prolific and interesting than most, makes rosés, and both old and young reds. And there's yet another style in the offing, tested by **Bodegas Egli**. Bobal is the leading grape in Utiel-Requena, it was planted widely in the nineteenth century for its colour and strength in the making of bulk wines. The area acted as a warehouse for local and foreign companies (mainly Swiss), that used it to improve their own wines. In previous centuries Bobal had spread into Horta de Valencia, Camp de Morvedre and Camp de Turia (many villages have plots of Bobal in the parish: Estivella, Paiporta, a village in Montroi and a hill in Morella).

Jaume Roig in *El Llibre de les dones* ("The Book of Women")[1] wrote that to plant a vine one should choose the healthy "muntalbana, boval negrella" varieties in order to obtain plentiful and good quality grapes, and he was right, those are the characteristics of the Bobal, bountifulness and virtue. They are also what the bulk producer provides, as the raw material used to improve wines of greater renown needs to be first-rate rather than mediocre. **Gracel** is 100 percent Bobal,[2] from vines that are over sixty years old, which gives it that attractively mature quality. It has a deep, fragrant aroma, and is silky and full in the mouth. Its nose has the sweet scent of mature tannins from old vines, which with their scant fruit (1.5 kg per vine) concentrate all their qualities in each grape. Ochando has given the wine three months in barrels of new French and American oak to emphasize these traits. This has come out just right, and has rounded out further with time – a year – in bottle. **Gracel** is an elegant and noble red wine, clean-tasting and with a balanced aftertaste. Bobal reds are achieving well-deserved acknowledgement. Tom Stevenson in his *World Wine Encyclopedia* (Reader's Digest, 1988) deems them tender and agreeable, the very virtues indicated by Jaume Roig six centuries previously. Oz Clarke, the great English winetaster, says that it makes good reds, strong and characterful, with plenty of grass and fruit. This is a fitting judgement for this noble red grape that is ready to take its place in the glasses of winelovers to reveal both its own magnificence and that of the people who grow it.

Website: None
Label: Gracel tinto 2000
Type: Tinto media crianza
ABV: 13%
Grape: Bobal
Approx. price: NA
Bodega: Enotec
Address: Avda. Lamo de Espinosa,32-E, 46340
Requena, Valencia
Tel: 962301744
Fax: 962304245
Email: enotec@infonegocio.com

NOTES

[1] Jaume Roig (d. 1478) was a Valencian physician and author of *L'Espill* (The Mirror) also known as *Llibre de les Dones* (Book of Women), a unique work of episodic narrative in 16,359 short verses detailing the intrinsic perversity of the female sex.

[2] This wine is unfortunately no longer being made.

Gran Fondillón:
The Saga Continues
Bodegas A. y M. Navarro, Villena (DO Alicante)

Since **Fondillón** first reappeared in 1976 (from the 1959 harvest) this wine has continued to make headway towards reestablishing its former glory. Others have followed in the wake of Salvador Poveda, the bodega that resurrected this wine. Bodegas Brotons and Bodegas Alfonso (now closed) in El Pinós; **Bocopa**, with its magnificent **Fondillón Alone**; and, of course, **Primitivo Quiles** in Monóver, who keep the memory of **Fondillón** alive in the huge barrels of their "solera". **Bodega Valle del Carche** and **El Sequé** also have **Fondillones** in progress, which we will be able to taste in a few years, after the lengthy ageing process in 1,800 litre Alicante "botas" (barrels) that this wine requires. The family of **Fondillones** has a new member in **Bodegas A. y M. Navarro** in Villena. Their **Gran Fondillón** is a classic. It has that light red, bright, vinegary colour (over fifteen years in barrel precipitate and send to the bottom – "fondillo" – of the barrel all the colouring and other matter that constitute the "mother" of the aged wine). It is this "fondillo" in the enormous barrels that is the root of – and gives name to – **Fondillón**.

Once a fixture on royal tables, as described by Saint-Simon and others, **Fondillón** was lost when phylloxera destroyed Europe's vines. Alicante became the wine provider for the affected areas, as it was the last place in Europe to be reached by the pest. All the Monastrell that could be harvested fetched a good price, and so was no longer kept for the lengthy ageing this wine requires. The body that might have protected it, the 1510 "Junta d'inhibició del vi foraster d'Alacant" (the "Board for the exclusion of foreign wine from Alicante" – the first **DO** set up anywhere in Europe), had ceased to exist in 1834 by virtue of a tax-hungry decree from Madrid. This had been one of the few regional "fueros" (rights) that remained after the draconian Nova Planta of Philip V at the end of the War of the Spanish Succession, and might have helped regulate the market during the late nineteenth-century boom. At such a time a body based on the idea of authenticity of origin would have been helpful.

Gran Fondillón from **Bodegas A. y M. Navarro** is beautifully presented. The best part of all is, of course, inside the bottle. It has a deep, subtly suggestive bouquet of almonds, and tastes of ripe figs alongside the classic cinnamon spice of this long-lived wine, with its distinctive bar-rel-aged character making it both dry and sweet at the same time. The aroma of Virginia tobacco is another classic Fondillón trait. It is a wine to be enjoyed over the prolonged end of a meal, once drunk with biscuits, or honeyed sweetmeats like the legendary Almoixavenes (a kind of baked doughnut). The recovery of this wine has been an epic, almost Biblical journey. Something lost in the mists of time, recovered and reborn to the delight of those who lament the extinction of any species. There has been a lot of faith behind the recovery of this wine, despite the disasters and difficulties along the way. It is to be hoped that the religious conflicts of our time can similarly be transformed into peaceful harmony. For those of us who fought to protect and promote **Fondillón** the struggle seemed to echo the words of the Psalm: "Behold, he who keeps Israel will neither slumber nor sleep." Let it not be forgotten, **Fondillón** is part of our universal heritage.

Website: www.aymnavarro.com
Label: Gran Fondillón 1964
Type: Fondillón
ABV: 15%
Approx price: €42
Bodega: A y M. Navarro
Address: Pintor Juan Gris 26, 03400 Villena, Alicante
Tel: 965801486
Fax: 965800978
Email: direccion@aymnavarro.com

Gran Imperial:
Sweet Wine
Primitivo Quiles, Monòver (DO Alicante)

The bodega of **Primitivo Quiles** in Monòver are among the old-est in the **Comunidad Valenciana**. Established in the late nine-teenth century, they continued a century-old tradition that began in near-by El Pinós and moved subsequently to Monòver. Everything about this bodega conveys classicism and tradition, a Monòver bodega in the time-honoured style. If anyone wants to know what Alicante wines were like before modern winemaking, this is the place to come. The wines are well-known: the classic **Raspay Brut**, a dark, thick wine of 14% ABV – dense, fragrant, spicy – is a rich wine to accompany meat or "arroz cal-doso"; the ever popular **Cono 4**, so named because it was kept in a great wooden cone-shaped cask (number 4) which can still be seen in the bode-ga. There is also a "rosado virgen" (free-run rosé – the juice runs off the vat without any pressing) made with Monastrell, as Primitivo's sworn covenant with this wine is sacred: "not a drop of red wine enters my bodega unless it's Monastrell," used to be his motto. He also makes a La Marina Moscatel and a white wine that puts hair on men's chests and curves on women. It has some even more traditional wines, like the **Moscatel extra-extra**, a **Mistela** made from grapes that are just about raisins, giving a dark, dense and ever so sweet wine; there is also **Fondillón El Abuelo**, the Alicante wine par excellence. But Primitivo's best wine, the jewel in his crown, is **Gran Imperial**, a sweet Monastrell, aged in the "solera" system (moving the wines from different vintages through various levels of butts to allow the young wines to acquire the qualities of the older ones), which is truly old, "longevo" as Primitivo likes to say. **Gran Imperial** is a noble dessert wine, rich on account of its tannins and its 10 grams of residual sugar, which after ageing in an old solera becomes fully aged, rounded, complete. **Gran Imperial** is the ideal wine with which to end a good meal, one of the best dessert wines in the world. It has given me some of the same joys and feelings as a great vin-tage Port, a mature Madeira or even a **Fondillón**. Its aroma of spiced cinammon and cloves with roast Virginia tobacco intermingling with a Havana cigar from the Vuelta Abajo valley itself. It is generous, elegant and weighty, with a hint of ripe figs, liquorice and cocoa. This wine is an excellent digestif – whatever the wining or the dining. **Gran Imperial** is a revitalizing tonic, too. This great wine reminds me of W.B. Yeats who, like me, loved two things: Ireland and dessert wines. We should emulate his words, "I sat and mused and drank sweet wine."[1]

Website: www.primitivoquiles.com
Label: Gran Imperial
Type: Sweet Monastrell aged in solera
ABV: 16%
Grape: Monastrell
Approx. price: €70
Bodega: Primitivo Quiles. Calle Mayor, 4. 03640 Monòver, Alicante
Tel: 965470099
Fax: 966960235
Email: info@primitivoquiles.com

NOTES

[1] William Butler Yeats, "The Madness of King Goll" (1889).

Heretat de Taverners:
The Reserva
Heretat de Taverners, Fontanars (DO Valencia)

Fontanars dels Alforins has established itself as a winemaking landmark over the last decade. This is due to the excellent climate and soil conditions (fabulous loamy soil and good rainfall levels), and also to the appearance of bodegas in the wake of Manuel Olaechea's setting up of the organic **Dominio de los Pinos** (see pages 30 and 78). In all these undertakings Daniel Belda, one of the great winemakers to have emerged in the **Comunidad Valenciana**, has acted as technical adviser. In his own bodega, Belda makes some interesting reds, and he has the distinction of being the moving force behind the rediscovery of the Verdil grape (see page 34), with which he has made some delightful white wines despite its difficult nature, in defiance of the neat categorization beloved of winemaking theory. The name of Daniel Belda will be linked forever with Fontanars.

The author was called in to participate in the interesting Heretat de Taverners project. This wine is made on the Taverners "**finca**", owned by the Montes-Reig family, with twenty-five **hectares** under vine: Cabernet Sauvignon, Tempranillo, Monastrell, Merlot and Graciano (that most aristocratic of Rioja grapes). The name Taverners is associated with a beautiful birch tree ("vern" in Valencian) that grows on the farm, also known as Casas de Colaus, a neoclassical gem dating from 1782. The "**finca**" is a proper château, with vineyards surrounding the house and its modern bodega with its ageing cellar containing barriques of several types of French and American oak.

Heretat de Taverners 2000 is a no-holds-barred **reserva**. It is made with Cabernet Sauvignon, Tempranillo and Monastrell. The first two are sharp, tannic grapes and Monastrell is robust and full-bodied. They make an excellent blend, but it needs the touch of a good winemaker, as they have separate maturing cycles, and though they combine well to start with, in barrel one variety will accelerate the oxidation of the others, making it very important to use new white oak to help the grapes to blend. The bouquet is exquisite, with aromas of truffle and green peppers, raspberry and ripe cherries. This wine has Daniel Belda's hallmark – as Vicent Montes says: "Daniel tastes the wines and then decides to give them more time in barrel" (fourteen to sixteen months here rather than the required twelve). **Heretat de Taverners** is a wine made by people who love both wine and Fontanars, in a way conveyed in that volcanic drinker Malcolm Lowry's poem "Without the Nighted Wyvern" (also known as "We Sit Unhackled Drunk and Mad to Edit"):[1]

> Notions of freedom are tied up with drink.
> Our ideal life contains a tavern

Website: www.heretatdetaverners.com
Label: Heretat de Taverners reserva 2000
Type: reserva
ABV: 13%
Grapes: Cabernet Sauvignon, Tempranillo, Monastrell
Approx. price: €8
Bodega: Casa Colaus, Crta. Fontanars Moixent, km. 1.8, 46635 Fontanars dels Alforins, Valencia
Tel: 962222294
Fax: 962222298
Email: info@heretatdetaverners.com

NOTES

[1] Malcolm Lowry (1909–57) was a writer and alcoholic. His masterpiece is the semi-autobiographical novel *Under the Volcano* (1947).

La Noria Crianza:
Organic Excellence
La Noria, Las Cuevas de Utiel (DO Utiel-Requena)

The **Comunidad Valenciana** is far outstripped by Andalusia and Extremadura when it comes to organic farming. In this region the organic movement has failed to establish itself as might have been expected, given the primacy of the countryside in Valencia's self-image. An environment under threat, the abuse of the countryside by its own inhabitants and an organic agriculture restricted mainly to unirrigated land, suggests that this self-image is largely myth. One sector that has responded enthusiastically to organic principles is wine. **La Noria crianza** 2000 is an organic wine produced by the "**finca**" of the same name in Las Cuevas de Utiel. It belongs to a family that owns one of the city of Valencia's top hotels. **La Noria** is a very beautiful wine domaine (with a neoclassical building in the Central European style dating from 1897) with a modern bodega.

They must have heeded the words of Frona Eunice Wait Colburn, "Planting a vineyard and making wine is a gentleman's occupation, and the highest type of agriculture."[1] **La Noria crianza** is an organic wine overseen by the Organic Farming Committee of the Comunidad Valenciana. Organic farming is the logical continuation of the philosophy of place of origin established in the nineteenth century to safeguard natural processes and the place of production of foodstuffs. During some excellent debates in July 2003 organized by the then director general of the Agriculture Council of the Valencian government, Auxiliadora Hernández, a significant ideological framework was drawn up to this end, but the agricultural sector was conspicuously absent (no sign of the **Denominación de Origen**, nor of the trade unions nor of business). The oft-invoked Valencia countryside is not minded to abandon intensive farming.

La Noria, on the other hand, has shown itself to be a highly worthwhile initiative. Aged in three different types of oak (French, American and Ukrainian), it is a perfect blend of Tempranillo and Bobal (50 percent of each), as the qualities of both grapes complement each other in barrel. A perfect blend, but not an easy one, as the grapes have different cycles. They even ripen and are picked several weeks apart and so are not vinified together. The Tempranillo brings good acidity and sharpness and

Bobal provides colour, alcohol and body, giving a full-bodied, wine with good fruit and oak.

Website: None
Label: La Noria crianza 2000
Type: Crianza tinto (organic)
ABV: 12.5%
Grapes: Tempranillo, Bobal
Approx. price: €6
Bodega: La Noria ECOVIN
Address: Ctra. Utiel-Camporrobles, Km 2, 46300 Utiel, Valencia
Tel: 96296563
Fax: 962963563
Email: vino@lanoria-ecovin.com

NOTES

[1] See Fernando Francés Chardonnay, Note 1, page 49.

Las Lomas:
Bobal "Nouveau"
Bodegas Schenk, Requena (DO Utiel-Requena)

The Swiss bodega Schenk began operating in Valencia eighty years ago seeking wines from the south for their colour and strength. In the 1980s they were among the pioneers of the renewal of Valencian wine with their Murviedro range. They have now extended to Requena, where Pablo Osorio, a creative and technically sophisticated winemaker, has created a new line of wines: **Las Lomas** and **Los Monteros**. The white **Los Monteros** – made from cold macerated Merseguera grapes and **carbonic maceration** fermented Moscatel de Alejandria – and the red **Corolilla Reserva** (100% Bobal), are notable for their intense aroma and fullness of flavour. **Las Lomas** is also exceptional, a red wine made in the same way as Beaujolais but with the Bobal grape. Every winemaking region in the world has had a go at making a Beaujolais-style wine, to be produced before Christmas and exhausted by San Blas (St Blaise, 3 February, patron saint of sore throats). But none have worked, except maybe in the Alava region of Rioja where a tradition of harvest wines existed, and Tempranillo grapes were macerated crudely in stone troughs. In the Valencia region the pioneers were the winemakers at **Bodegas Egli** in **Casa lo Alto**, who installed state-of-the-art containers (traditional wine vats are no good for genuine carbonic maceration). These winemakers (Ángel Guaita, Óscar Valero, Hilario Martínez, Santiago González, Sylvia Soler and Ludolfo Ortiz) led by Cristóbal Ruiz designed and produced an excellent nouveau wine, Villa Albosa, which sold very well in the UK through the prestigious and demanding Sunday Times Wine Club. Though it seemed at first that Tempranillo would be the most likely grape, in the end the choice was Bobal for its similarity to Beaujolais' Gamay grape, and its growth cycle (standard blooming and late ripening) ideal for the clean extraction of aromas and intensity of flavour. If they got it right straight off the bat, it was because a good winemaking culture teaches this sort of thing. Pablo also has this knowledge, as he too has made a nouveau-style red with Bobal, full of the scent of ripe fruit, and the exquisite taste of sweet tannins from ripe grapes. It has good body and strength, it could never be said that it was at all puny. **Las Lomas** is a long way from being merely a thirst-quencher as is sometimes the case with Beaujolais nouveau. This is due to a better climate in

Utiel-Requena than in mid-Burgundy, and to the variety used: Bobal, a masterstroke that suggests a new possibility for the wines of this area, the diversity of which is one of its great strengths.[1]

Website: www.murviedro.es
Label: Las Lomas tinto 2003
Type: joven nouveau
ABV: 12.5%
Grape: Bobal
Approx. price: NA
Bodega: Schenk Ampli
Address: Ampliación Polígono el Romeral, 46340 Requena, Valencia
Tel: 962329003
Fax: 962329002
Email: murviedro@murviedro.es

NOTES

[1] Sadly, this wine is no longer being made.

Laudum Organic Wine:
The Potential of the Vinalopó
Bocopa, Petrer (DO Alicante)

Organic farming is the answer to the violence inflicted on the environment, and it will help us to improve the way we eat. "Tell me what you eat and I will tell you what you are," said Brillat-Savarin,[1] and if his dictum holds true there is certainly cause for concern.

An organic wine follows natural processes for the vine and the wine. It is true that our southern climate is well-suited to organic farming, but sometimes the dryness and heat are both an opportunity and a threat. The Vinalopó valley has always been an arid zone, which is why the sixteenth-century Tibi reservoir was the first to be built in Europe and, together with the Knights Hospitallers' bridge over the Rhône, the most important civil engineering project of its time. The deforestation and loss of vegetation that it entailed adversely affected the local climate. Reforestation should be a priority of the regional government, both for our collective good and for the agriculture and the wines of this great valley. Both the technical capacity and EU funding have long existed for a reforestation project. The Vinalopó area has undiscovered winemaking potential, far greater than in days gone by. Today its reds are highly regarded, but more could be achieved if the hills and valleys were reforested. All the great winegrowing areas in the world, the Côtes du Rhône, Burgundy, Bordeaux, the Napa Valley, Stellenbosch, are forested. The relationship between trees and vines in order to achieve the noblest aromatic characteristics of a wine – fruits of the forest and aromatic herbs – have been demonstrated. Jean Lenoir, biologist and engineer, showed these relationships between places and aromas in his "book-object" *Le Nez du Vin* with its aromagrams, like that between Gewürztraminer and the forests of Alsace.[2] When you drink this red **Laudum** from **Bocopa** and enjoy the fullness of its natural bouquet, all clean aromas, with hints of thyme and basil and a sylvan touch of fresh sage, you embrace the magnificence of nature. **Laudum** is a young organic red wine with a powerful aroma of redcurrants and raspberries. It is made with Monastrell, Tempranillo and Cabernet Sauvignon, which are all vigorous varieties. The first is low in acidity, but high in oxidative capacity and residual sugar, while the rest have good astringency, acidity, longevity and are very dry. They make an excellent blend. This 2001 was brought out later than usual as fermentation was prolonged, especially malolactic fermentation, in order to give these natural processes their full scope. **Laudum** from **Bocopa** is a wine that conveys the potential of these "**comarcas**", their natural environment, their ancient wine traditions, their Mediterranean spirit, and a wine culture whose greatest tradition is a sheer love of wine. **Bocopa**, the bodega that makes it, is a modern and efficient **second-grade cooperative**, which makes other excellent wines like **Marina Alta**, the exquisite **Terreta Rosé** and a good **Fondillón, Alone**. They also produce **Sol de Alicante**, a Moscatel "vino de licor" named after one of the few things in life we can rely on.

Website: www.bocopa.com
Label: Laudum 2001.
Type: Tinto joven ecológico
ABV: 13.5%
Grapes: Monastrell, Cabernet Sauvignon, Tempranillo
Approx. price: €3–5
Bodega: Bocopa
Address: Paraje Les Pedreres, Autovia Alicante-Madrid, km. 200-201, 03610 Petrer, Alicante
Tel: 966950489
Fax: 966950406
Email: info@bocopa.com

NOTES

[1] "Le Nez du Vin" is a training kit to develop the "olfactive alphabet" and educate the sense of smell for wine tasting.

2 Jean Anthelme Brillat-Savarin (1755–1826), a French lawyer and politician, who gained fame as an epicure and gastronome through his great work published in 1825 at his own expense, *Physiologie du goût* (The Physiology of Taste), the impressive subtitle of which is *or, Meditations of transcendent gastronomy; a theoretical, historical and topical work, dedicated to the gastronomes of Paris by a professor, member of several literary and scholarly societies.*

Les Alcusses:
From California to Moixent
Celler del Roure, Moixent (DO Valencia)

One of the characteristics of the new generation of Valencian winemakers is the absence of any inferiority complex. They all have the same schooling and aspiration, a "**vino de alta expresión**", following in the footsteps of the stars from Priorat in Catalonia, with very different points of market reference to established wines. These are winemakers in search of their own style, like Samuel Beckett's characters waiting for Godot and some existential truth, combining new winemaking techniques with their own grape varieties and the local soils and climate. Pablo Calatayud – agricultural engineer and winegrower – set up a small winery, **Celler del Roure**, a few years ago in Moixent where his family has a furniture business. Here they make two wines: **Maduresa** and **Les Alcusses**. **Maduresa** is a more substantial wine, sturdier and made to stand up to other heavyweight wines, to which end he has reclaimed the forgotten local grape variety, Mandó. Many people consider this his best wine. I, however, lean towards **Les Alcusses**, which is more restrained, elegant and aromatic. If **Maduresa** is more in the line of a Priorat or a Ribera del Duero, **Les Alcusses** is a "Napa Valley". This does not mean that they are just like those wines – these have their own personality – but there is a common denominator. Pablo's winemaking reminds me of what I was taught by Salvatore Pablo Lucia, Professor in the Faculty of Medicine at the University of California and author of *Alcohol and Civilization* (McGraw-Hill, 1963), "wine is the most complex fluid in nature, apart from blood." Using Monastrell, Cabernet Sauvignon, Tempranillo and Syrah, he has made in **Les Alcusses** a blend along the lines of Californian Meritage. Consciously or unconsciously he has developed a style of wine in the mould of those developed in California in the 1960s. **Les Alcusses** 2002 has vibrancy, just the right amount of astringency, with scents of raspberry jam, green pepper, forest truffle and an underlying floral aroma (geraniums). The bouquet is balanced, combining plums and butter (like the great Pomerol), and spices – vanilla and cloves. **Les Alcusses** spends four months in French and American oak barrels. "Bâtonnage" (stirring the lees with a stick) was carried out during **maceration** to enhance this extraction of aromas and flavours, but the bountifulness of the wine comes from the trouble Pablo takes with the vines, this is pocket winemaking in every sense, not just because it involves minute attention to each and every vine, but also because it costs a fortune. The vineyards are not so much worked as gardened, with horticultural rather than agricultural tools. **Les Alcusses** will develop very well in bottle, it is an excellent wine for laying down that has something of the great Californian reds made by Robert Mondavi and Miguel Torres.

Website: None
Label: Les Alcusses 2002 tinto
Type: media crianza; 4 months in barrel
ABV: 13%
Grapes: Monastrell, Tempranillo, Cabernet Sauvignon, Syrah
Approx. price: €9–10
Bodega: Celler del Roure
Address: Ctra. Les Alcusses km. 2.5, 46640 Moixent, Valencia
Tel: 962295020
Fax: 962295142
Email: cellerdelroure@hotmail.com

Licor de Teulada:
Under Fire
Coop. Sant Vicent Ferrer, Teulada (DO Alicante)

Valencia is one of the historic distilling regions, to which the long tradition of **Mistelas** owes its existence. Arnau de Vilanova (Montpellier 1238–Genoa 1311), the Occitan doctor and alchemist, served the kings of Aragon (Pere II, Alfons II and Jaume II) in the thirteenth century. He operated in every corner of the kingdom of Aragon, but it was in the kingdom of Valencia that he spent most time, and where he gained his grounding in the Talmud. He wrote in Latin and Catalan, and was fluent in Arabic and Hebrew, making him familiar with the medical culture of these civilizations. Arnau de Vilanova left a groundbreaking treatise on winemaking and alchemy, the techniques of which are still in use.[1] If we think of Gay-Lussac and Pasteur as the fathers of modern oenology, Vilanova was the first technical winemaker.[2] Before him the process was empirical – people knew that something was happening, but not what – and after him they knew what was happening, but not how. We had to wait until Gay-Lussac to learn how the process occurred. Another ancestral line in the family tree of distillation consists of the military and monastic orders: the Knights Hospitaller, Knights Templar, Knights of Montesa, Benedictines and Carmelites all left a long list of *aqua vitae*, as the ancients called distilled alcohol. Desmond Seward wrote in *Monks and Wine*: "One of monasticism's greatest services to Western civilization has been its contribution to wine-growing and to the distillation of strong waters."[3] Their tradition was more important than that left by the Moors in the kingdom of Valencia, since though the latter were experts in the art of distilling, the prohibition of wine led them to use it in perfume and medicine. Arnau knew of that area of Islamic culture and of the alchemical knowledge of the Irish monks who had recovered the knowledge of the Alexandrian Greeks (it was the Greek Egyptian Zosimos of Panoplis who set up the first stable cold-still) and the Aristotelian treatises.

Once experts in "aguardientes" (aníses, brandies and moscatel liqueurs – oh! for that magnificent "Licor Carmelitano" once made in Benicàssim by monks from the Carmelite monastery in Desierto de las Palmas), little is left of Valencians' mastery of spirits. The heat of the still warmed Valencians during their golden age in the eighteenth century. One of those that survives is the "licor de Moscatell" from the **Cooperativa Sant Vicent Ferrer de Teulada** in la Marina (this cooperative gets its name from the fact that St Vincent's sister, Constanze, lived in this lovely town where her house still stands). The **licor de moscatel de Teulada** is a noble spirit made by distilling Moscatel wine according to an ancient local recipe. The **Teulada Moscatel** is grown on terraces looking out to sea in accordance with the rustic saying "qui de vinya plantar vol, procura li pegue el sol" ("he who wants to plant vines, make sure on them the sun shines").

Website: www.coop-santvicent.com
Label: Licor de Moscatell
Type: Distilled Moscatel
ABV: 17%
Grape: Moscatel
Approx. price: €10
Bodega: Cooperativa Agrícola Sant Vicent Ferrer
Address: Avda. Las Palmas, 32, 03725 Teulada, Alicante
Tel: 965740051
Fax: 965740489
Email: bodega@coop-santvicent.com

NOTES

[1] In *De aqua vitae simplici et composita* Arnau de Vilanova (1238–1311) explained how to derive spirits from wine and the corresponding medical applications of this "eau-de-vie" according to the signs of the zodiac that govern each organ.

[2] Joseph Louis Gay-Lussac (1778–1850) posed the following equation in 1815: "One molecule of sugar gives two molecules of ethyl alcohol and two molecules of carbon dioxide, as well as a strong emission of heat." Louis Pasteur (1822–95) demonstrated that if wine is gently heated to 60°C for a short time, the growth of harmful bacteria is prevented and the wine does not go sour in bottles or barrels.

[3] Desmond Seward, *Monks and Wine* (Mitchell Beazley, 1979).

Loma de Lanzas:
Absolutely Bobal
Bodegas Ejarque, El Rebollar (DO Utiel-Requena)

Every year more excellent new Bobal wines appear. From its bulk wine past when it was mainly sought for its blending qualities of colour, strength and stability, Bobal has become the hot new thing among wine lovers, won over by its quality, its personality and its elegant complexity. "Bobal of our dreams", as Carlos Delgado, editor of *MiVino* magazine, has referred to the grape (in issue 94, February 2005, see also www.mivino.info) is an apt expression for this Mediterranean red. Bobal is the leading variety in Utiel-Requena, or rather, **the** variety in this leading **DO**. It is coming on in leaps and bounds, after the triumph of Ribera del Duero in the 1980s, and Somontano and Priorat in the '90s, it is Utiel-Requena's turn. It could have come earlier, but some people's cognitive paralysis held things back. Delayed, but not prevented, as the qualities of Bobal and of Utiel-Requena continue to impose themselves to the extent that they cannot be denied by even those "connoisseurs" suffering from chronic "**Riojitis**-Riberitis influenza". Many people have backed this varietal to the hilt, such as Félix Cuartero, professor at the Requena Wine School, with all his experience, and Pedro Beltrán whose **Campo Arcis** is a Bobal **reserva** from old vines with an exquisite bouquet of fine butter and English toffee.

Loma de Lanzas 2001 is 100 percent Bobal made from old vines. It is the best wine made by **Bodegas Ejarque**,[1] who make other worthy reds and a silky **barrel-fermented** Chardonnay. **Loma de Lanzas** 2001 spent 18 months in medium-grain American oak barrels from the oak forests of the Napa Valley and Missouri. It is an intense, though evolved, garnet red (moving from dense to brilliant and back). As you would expect from a wine from old vines from which the grapes have been picked at full ripeness, there are fruit aromas of blueberries and even lychees alongside polished tannins from the oak. In the mouth it is slightly viscous, spicy (vanilla) with a touch of astringency. Here is a very good wine that should not be overlooked.

The progress of Bobal wines has been remarkable, but some things have been lost on the way over the last decade, during which few people saw the grape's possibilities, beyond the pioneers and the regulatory authority. Many vines were ripped out, due to the variety's low yield. The fault lies with some regional ministers of agriculture who failed to develop a strategic plan, and in consequence a valuable heritage of vineyards and wines was lost. The quiescent attitude of the powers that be is reminiscent of Sherlock Holmes' exchange in the story "Silver Blaze":

"Is there any point to which you would wish to draw my attention?"
"To the curious incident of the dog in the night-time."
"The dog did nothing in the night-time."
"That was the curious incident."[1]

Website: None
Label: Loma de Lanzas 2001
Type: Tinto Reserva.
ABV: 13%
Grape: Bobal
Approx. price: €9
Bodega: Ejarque
Address: Calle de Yátova, 10, 46391 Rebollar, Valencia
Tel: 916508344
Fax: 962300949
Email: lalcacer@infonegocio.com

NOTES

[1] This Bobal wine is now marketed by the bodega under a different name, its own, as **Bodegas Ejarque crianza**.

Los Pinos:
The Organic "Château"
Los Pinos, Fontanars (DO Valencia)

Fontanars is a wine-growing haven. It all began with Manuel Olaechea (see also page 30), a Peruvian who fell in love over fifteen years ago with the flatness and character of this place (having travelled throughout France, Portugal and Spain) and its microclimate, one of the best in the **Comunidad Valenciana**. Fontanars, which stands 700 metres above sea level, has excellent loamy soil and a high water level. It has always done well for itself – whatever has been sown here has flourished. It is here that Olaechea set up **Los Pinos** as a wine domaine, a château in the classic French style, with the intention of making organic wine. As a young man on his father's cotton estate he experimented successfully with organic methods. A bumper crop one year, which coincided happily with high market prices, was followed by a Biblical plague that destroyed the harvest and threatened the plants themselves, all the previous year's revenue was spent in an unsuccessful search for a solution. Then he went to Berkeley, California, where pioneering techniques in organic agriculture had been developed and they advised synchronizing the natural cycle of the pests' predators with the plagues. This affected him profoundly, and when he set up **Dominio de los Pinos** he knew that it would have to be organic. He created a bodega surrounded by vines, and there he grows, produces and creates an interesting range of organic wines which he sells with greater success around the world than he does at home, despite their excellence. In **Los Pinos** he grows Cabernet Franc, Cabernet Sauvignon, Merlot and Monastrell, for the reds. And with Malvasía, Muscat Blanc à Petits Grains, Sauvignon Blanc and Viognier, the noble white grape of the Côtes du Rhône, he makes interesting and remarkable whites: his **Selección** and **Cum Laude**. The red **crianza** 2000 is a marvel of vanilla and green pepper, dark fruits (black cherries mixed with morello cherries). It is lively in the mouth, slightly grassy, with a hint of toast (possibly roast chestnuts) and fresh figs. **Los Pinos** is a wine for laying down, as two tastings over seven months show it to be continuing to develop very well. Olaechea and his winemaker Omar have given it one year in oak – more than the regulations require. French and American casks help the Monastrell, with its tendency to oxidize, blend with the long-lived and astringent Cabernet. The organic initiative is always welcome, the alternative to respecting the environment is so bleak that we cannot carry on without greater ecological engagement. As Gore Vidal has pointed out,[1] before there were many things and few people, now there are many people and few things. It is a question of ethics not quantity.

Website: None
Label: Los Pinos tinto 2000
Type: Crianza
ABV: 13%
Grapes: Cabernet Sauvignon, Merlot, Monastrell
Approx. price: €8–10
Bodega: Dominio Los Pinos
Address: Casa Los Pinos s/n, 46635 Fontanars dels Alforins, Valencia.
Tel: 962222090
Fax: 962222086
Email: domlospinos@telefonica.net

NOTES

[1] Gore Vidal (b. 1925) is a writer and waspish critic of US politics.

Maduresa:
Triumph of the Will
Celler del Roure, Moixent (DO Valencia)

Celler del Roure in Moixent is a small bodega that makes the best red in the whole of the Valencia **DO** (see page 72). The bodega's second wine, **Les Alcusses**, is the dark horse because their top wine, **Maduresa**, is more heavy-hitting, but it is less finished than **Les Alcusses**, whose elegance has seduced a legion of followers of cosmopolitan palate. Why has **Les Alcusses** garnered a more discerning audience than **Maduresa**, which is also more expensive? It is due to the definition of style, perfectly achieved in **Les Alcusses**, but less so in the first vintages of **Maduresa**.

The definition of style is the most important quality of a wine and a measure of quality. In some bodegas this comes about because they have received for their first wine the blessing of influential commentators, the best known and most influential being, without a doubt, Robert Parker. I look at Parker's point-rankings and I can see that he rates with good sense and fairness, but these are not the only great wines, just the ones he likes and rewards. **Maduresa** is certainly a wine made with loving care, by precision winemaking (as is the case with **Les Alcusses**) but the end result is not the same. Why should this be? The first reason is that until recently the external consultants used by Pablo Calatayud were leading **Maduresa** down a dead-end street, because this new breed of wine consultants has a problem, they apply a one-size-fits-all model, but when they operate in a particular area they do not know the parameters and behaviour of the soil, the climate and the grape varieties. The second reason is that the ripening cycle of the grape and its **maceration** during vinification were not in harmony, and the wine's conductibility with the barrels used must have left a retrospective mark on the fermentation. This was why the 2002 **Maduresa** frustrated its maker, Pablo Calatayud, an honest man who loves wine. He decided that from then on he would take **Maduresa** into his own hands, as he already did with **Les Alcusses**, which is totally his in every respect. His iron will and winemaker's fighting spirit have rewarded him with a great wine.

Maduresa 2003 is the best wine to have come out of **Celler del Roure**, achieving a rating of 93 points from Robert Parker, and this wine does have the definition and excellence of a minutely worked "grand vin". **Maduresa** 2003 is a symphony of aromas of wild ripe fruit: black plums, strawberries and raspberries with an elegant touch of violet. It is best of all in the mouth, with a touch of cinnamon, toasted oak, a luxurious dab of butter (as if from contented Irish cows) and an elusive hint of liquorice in the finish, which suggests itself with each swirl of the glass after pouring, and is a mark of the nobility of this wine. **Maduresa** 2003 gets top points for the warm toast of its wood, good well-made French casks from the best oak trees in central France. This is the best **Maduresa** so far, but not the best that will be made. The percentage of the grapes underpinning its excellence, Syrah and the local Mandó, ought to grow at the expense of the Monastrell and Cabernet Sauvignon. Pablo's sensitive judgement will provide us in future vintages with an iconic red wine, as he has done already with **Les Alcusses** (one of the twenty-five best wines in all Spain). **Maduresa** is the living embodiment of that quest of Voltaire's for "A wine to be drunk in the hope that it will never finish."[1]

Website: None
Label: Maduresa 2003
Type: Tinto de Reserva
ABV: 14%
Grapes: Syrah, Cabernet Sauvignon, Mandó, Monastrell, Merlot, Petit Verdot
Approx. price: €16–18
Bodega: Celler del Roure
Address: Ctra. de Les Alcusses, km 2.5, 46640 Moixent, Valencia
Tel: 962295020
Fax: 962295142
Email: cellerdelroure@hotmail.com

NOTES

[1] Voltaire (1694–1778) was an Enlightenment writer, intellectual and satirist. His real name was François-Marie Arouet.

Megala:
The Future of La Costera
Bodegas Enguera, Enguera (DO Valencia)

From Enguera to Fontanars dels Alforins and from Moixent to La Font de la Figuera, the whole Clariano **subzone**, a winegrowing area in the heart of the Valencia **DO,** has been making prodigious progress in terms of quality and definition. Clariano encompasses various winegrowing localities from "**comarcas**" such as La Vall d'Albaida, La Canal de Navarrés and La Costera, which produce red wines that manage to be both cosmopolitan and local at the same time, not unlike certain appellations of the Rhône Valley, particularly the Côte Rôtie (covering 200 **hectares**) and Côtes de Rhône-Villages (5,000 **hectares**). But the wild herbs, terraces and hillsides of these "**comarcas**" are not the only parallels, the Syrah and Monastrell (known as Mourvèdre in the Rhône, since it reached France from Sagunto, formerly called Morvedre), are another shared feature, and the character of Clariano is improved and defined by such varietals as **Garnacha Tintorera**, Garnacha and the local Mandó. The **subzone** has an extraordinary roster of bodegas: **Heretat de Taverners, Fernando Francés, Cooperativa La Viña, Daniel Belda, Los Pinos** and **Enguera**, all producers of good wines that are much sought after by possessors of discerning wallets and even finer palates. **Bodegas Enguera** is a young bodega that makes limited amounts of good quality red wine of distinct personality in a modern style. It is a well-run operation led by a highly professional oenologist, Chema García de la Cuadra, who has produced a very elegant red wine.

Since he is a young and well-trained new wave winemaker, he has made a modern red wine in that image, all winemaking flair shorn of inhibitions and complexes. His **Megala** red comes in at 14.5% ABV and spends thirteen months in French oak casks, but in neither case is this overly noticeable, wherein lies its elegance. Made with fifty per cent each of Syrah and Monastrell, it is a perfect blend which is marked slightly by the youth of the Syrah vines. Monastrell produces very structured wines after just a few years, but the Syrah vines need more time to mature, which is an advantage for **Megala**, as each vintage is going to be better than its predecessor, something that not everyone can say, even the greatest bodegas. I like this red wine, not only for the smooth elegance of its bouquet, but also for its vermilion colour and intense violet nose, so characteristic of Syrah. The Monastrell is the queen of this blend with intense but controlled tannins and its full-blooded cinnamon and clove spiciness. It is ready for drinking now, and it will also keep for a couple of years, during which it will evolve and develop intriguingly. **Bodegas Enguera** is further confirmation of the potential of the Clariano **subzone**, which has the highest concentration of quality red wines in the Valencia **DO**. Manuel López Alejandre, secretary of the Montilla-Moriles **DO**, admires and reflects on the present and future of Valencian wine in the light of its climate, its soil and its winemaking expertise. This evangelist for wine and its culture who succeeded, after a prolonged struggle, in rescuing the wines of Montilla-Moriles from the severe crisis that overtook that region in the 1980s, insists with all his wine wisdom that it is in the deepening of the Mediterranean values of these wines that their tradition and modernity will be enshrined.

Website: www.bodegasenguera.com
Label: Megala 2003
Type: tinto de crianza
ABV: 14.5%
Grapes: Monastrell, Syrah
Approx. price: €8–10
Bodega: Bodegas Enguera
Address: Chalet del Rio, s/n, 46810 Enguera, Valencia
Tel: 961364166
Fax: 961364167
Email: bodega@cessa.es

Mestizaje:
Independent Wine
Bodega Mustiguillo (Vino de la Tierra El Terrerazo)

Antonio Sarrión set up **Bodegas Mustiguillo** on land in Las Cuevas, where he makes his **"alta expresión"** reds: **Quincha Corral**, **Finca Terrerazo** (see page 50) and latterly **Mestizaje**. These have two characteristics, the vines of the **"comarca"**, and the techniques associated with **"alta expresión"** wines. The first wines he brought out (**Quincha Corral** and **Finca del Terrerazo**) were notable for their consistency and weight. **Mustiguillo** opted from the first to remain outside the area's **Denominación de Origen**, since it wants to be an independent "vino de la tierra".

Their reds are based on the Bobal grape in which Antonio has placed his trust, with some Cabernet Sauvignon and Tempranillo, changing the proportions for the **Terrerazo** and the **Quincha Corral**. I tasted these three times over a year and they improved every time, but for me they have yet to achieve their full definition, by which I mean their wine style. I know they are great wines, and wine guru Robert Parker has given them a high rating (95 points to **Quincha Corral**, the highest ever achieved by a Valencian wine). These are quite some wines, but to my winemaking mind and battered old palate there is something missing. It could be that Antonio is right, and after the intense **maceration** to which they have been subjected in order to achieve that heady aroma they need time in bottle to arrive at their full potential. However, **Mestizaje**, his third wine, is a different animal altogether. Sarrión says he made it to show that a fine red wine can be made from young vines, and how!, though life is easier working with old vines. Sarrión is looking for a more malleable wine in order to achieve that distinctive **Mustiguillo** style. This can be seen in the fact that whereas the first two wines are made with three grapes, **Mestizaje** is made with no fewer than six. The key is in the different styles of wines that are being merged – there is a Bordeaux-Rioja style (Cabernet Sauvignon, Merlot and Tempranillo), a powerful Côtes du Rhône (Syrah) and a Priorat (Bobal and **Garnacha Tintorera**).

Blending six different varieties is hard work, and you have to be a good winemaker, but harmonizing three different styles is still more complex, and you have also to be a good winegrower, and have a good technical infrastructure. Sarrión has all this. His bodega is housed in lovely neoclassical rural edifices set in a charming estate. **Mestizaje** is an outstanding red wine at 13.5% ABV, with moderate acidity and heaps of fruit aromas (raspberries, blueberries and plums). There is a hint of green pepper, a bit of grassiness and spice (vanilla, cloves and toasted cinnamon), the wood is present but not overpowering, which is to be expected, since Sarrión does not skimp on the euros when it comes to buying his elegant barrels from only the finest suppliers.

website: None
Label: Mestizaje tinto 2002
Type: vino de guarda de crianza
ABV: 13.5%
Grapes: Bobal, Tempranillo, Cabernet Sauvignon, Merlot, Syrah, Garnacha Tintorera
Approx. price: €9–11
Bodega: Mustiguillo
Address: Ctra. N-330 km 195, 46300 El Terrerazo, Las Cuevas de Utiel, Valencia
Tel: 962304575
Fax: 962301964
Email: info@bodegamustiguillo.com

Mistelanova:
A Luminous Moscatel
Coop. de Montserrat, Montserrat (DO Valencia)

Oranges and the Moscatel grape are the symbolic fruits of traditional Valencian imagery. This grape came to Valencia from Alexandria in the first century AD. During the period of Muslim dominance it was the only wine grape that was not ripped out, thanks to its use as a fruit and for raisins. Today there are almost 5,000 **hectares** of Moscatel in La Marina, La Foia de Bunyol, La Ribera Alta and La Plana, with more grown in three other "**comarcas**". Along with Moscatel, the Romans brought the first distilling techniques, which were already known in Greece (Aristotle had described them), but which did not work well due to the instability of the early stills. It was Zosimos of Panoplis, the Egyptian Greek alchemist of the fourth century AD, who developed techniques to stabilize the process. **Mistela** is one of the ancient Greek wines still with us, along with vermouth and retsina. These, given the primitive winemaking techniques, needed the addition of roots, herbs or spirits. The "mistelization" of a wine consists in adding a proportion of alcohol to the grape juice to stop fermentation, so preventing the sugar present in the must from turning to ethanol. So **Mistela** is always sweet. The best Moscatel **Mistela** in the **Comunidad Valenciana**, which is to say the whole Mediterranean, is from the Montserrat cooperative. They have specialized in the production of a "white **Mistela**" of exquisite aroma, as pale, transparent and limpid as the light at dawn. This is itself an achievement, as some make the mistake of sweetening and darkening their **Mistela**, which is naturally light in colour, made as it is with white grapes. This tendency, now less common, was often the result of inadequate winemaking knowledge, and the response to any suggestion that they were in error was to say that it was the traditional way, which is quite something in a region like Valencia where all but militant cultural nationalists have forsaken historical memory. Moscatel **Mistela** is an important part of Valencia's cultural heritage. Additionally, it is the only Valencian wine with a captive market. At every food and wine fair it is the first to run out ("What do you mean there's no misteleta!"), and no home is without a drop to offer guests. That is why it is so important to make it naturally, pale, as they do in Montserrat. Mistelanova is a fresh, aromatic, sweet "vino de licor", which is like biting into a Moscatel grape fresh off the vine. It goes very well with foie gras and pâtés. It is ideal for rounding off a meal instead of the spirit shots of dubious origin that restaurant-goers are routinely offered. **Mistelanova** is an elixir of life, as is reflected in the old saying: "El vi fa sang i l'aigua fang" ("Wine makes blood and water mud").

Website: None
Label: Mistelanova
Type: Mistela
ABV: 15%
Grape: Moscatel de Alejandría
Approx. price: €3
Bodega: Sociedad Cooperativa V. Agrovinícola de Monserrat
Address: Calle Dr Marañón s/n, 46192 Montserrat, Valencia
Tel/Fax: 962999042
Email: monserrat@fecoav.es

Mistela Vittore:
The Great Tradition
Bodegas Valsangiacomo, Chiva (DO Valencia)

There is probably a bottle of **Mistela** somewhere in a cupboard in every Valencian household, the only Valencian wine with a captive market – its own. Though **Mistela** can be made from just about every sort of wine, the Moscatel of Alexandria grape (also known as the Valencia or Roman Moscatel) makes the sweetest and best.

Valencian **Mistela**, too, has been has touched by modernity, and for over a decade it has been made naturally, growing more elegant, pale and fragrant like the best Moscatels in the world: from Beaumes de Venise, Frontigan and St-Jean-de-Minervois in France, and from San Joaquin Valley in California. A fortunate side-effect of this has been virtually to drive out the bad habit of darkening **Mistela** with burnt caramel. Though there are also naturally dark Moscatels, the darkness coming from harvesting the grapes late, which in a golden, amber-skinned variety such as Moscatel produces a dark honey-coloured **Mistela**. Only three remain of this darker type: **Carmelitano del Desierto de las Palmas** in la Plana, **Primitivo Quiles' Moscatel Extra Cremat**, and **Mistela Vittore de Moscatel** from **Bodegas Valsangiacomo**. This hundred-year old bodega has its origins in Italian-speaking Switzerland – from Ticino, where there is another Bodega Valsangiacomo that belongs to another branch of the family.

This bodega produces a line of modern-style bottled wines, but it has also stayed in the bulk-selling trade. It is really three companies in one – a bulk seller, a modern bottled-wine producer and also a maker of traditional, even cult, wines, like its **Mistela**, and its wonderful "antica formula" Vermouth. **Mistela Vittore** is a dark brown honey-scented "vino de licor", very dense, fragrant and yet fruity, with hints of walnut and Valencian "chufa". It has a lovely sweet taste and would round off a meal better than those little glasses of dubious origin best described by Shakespeare in Sonnet 119:

What potions have I drunk of Siren tears
Distill'd from limbecks foul as hell within

Mistelas, on the other hand, are the embodiment of Mediterranean civilization. They are an ancient product of the classical Mediterranean, and of all the countries on its coast, Valencia's **Mistela** is the finest, though they need to keep half an eye on their markets and the other half on certain appellations in the south of France, between Roussillon and Montpellier, and watch out for the magnificent sweet wines being produced there. The international market knows all about Valencian **Mistelas**, both modern and traditional, such as **Vittore**, which has won medals at the International Wine Challenge in London. This is no small achievement, as it is up against the finest sweet wines. This **Moscatel Vittore** is worthy of the noble and beautiful lines by Cavafy, a fellow-countryman of Aristotle, the first European to write about the process of distilling:

> "What distillate can be discovered from herbs
> of a witching brew," said an aesthete,
> "what distillate prepared according
> to the formulas of ancient Grecosyrian magi...[1]

Website: www.cherubino.es
Label: Moscatel Vittore
Type: Mistela, vino de licor
ABV: 15%
Grape: Moscatel de Alejandría
Approx. price: €3–4
Bodega: Valsangiacomo
Address: Carretera Cheste-Godelleta, km 1, 46370 Chiva, Valencia
Tel: 962510861
Fax: 962511361
Email: cherubino@cherubino.es

NOTES

[1] Constantine Cavafy, "According To The Formulas Of Ancient Grecosyrian Magi" (1931).

Montcabrer:
The Wine from the Mountain
Vins del Comtat, Cocentaina (DO Alicante)

El Comtat, previously a wine-producing locality, lost this aspect of its identity with the arrival of the phylloxera pest in 1907. It was the last place in Europe to have its wines destroyed by the plague. The phylloxera parasite arrived from North America in 1870, coming in through Bordeaux, Malaga and Oporto with American vines.

When phylloxera arrived at Cocentaina, the solution to the epidemic had already been discovered (grafting European vines onto the parasite-resistant American rootstock). But here the arrival of phylloxera coincided with a collapse in demand from elsewhere, as their vines were restored. Here they were not replanted and you can still see the terraces where the vines were grown prior to the arrival of phylloxera.

Vins del Comtat de Cocentaina decided to change this, and although they began in 1996 as an artisanal operation, the bodega now produces 200,000 bottles a year. They make a sweet Moscatel, two dry white Moscatels – one "joven" and one barrel-aged –- from vines in the Valle del Lliber, and red wines from international varietals: Syrah, Cabernet Sauvignon, Merlot, Tempranillo and Monastrell as well as the local Giró (Garnacha). This is the local variety, just as in La Marina, a locality with which the grape is more closely associated than here in the Vinalopó. Giró is a variety that, when using old vines and mountain wine-growing methods, produces spicy, mature, rich and complex wines. It is also grown in Mallorca, Priorat and California – where it was taken from Mallorca by the Franciscan Friar Junípero de Serra when he went to found the California missions in the 1760s (see page 21) – and is known as Giró and Gironet. **Vins del Comtat** use this interesting grape in their Penya Cadiella red, blending it very well with Merlot, Syrah and Cabernet Sauvignon. Their best wine is **Montcabrer**, a powerful Cabernet Sauvignon monovarietal that is elegant in the mouth after spending ten months in French oak barrels and another four in American, a particularly effective combination for working with Cabernet Sauvignon's astringency and longevity. Fine grained wood and slow oxigenation for the first ten months and then a short blast of powerful American wood to round things off before calming things down again in bottle. **Montcabrer** is a wine with 13.7% ABV and over 2.5 grams of residual sugar per litre (unfermented sugar in the grape juice or must), which gives the wine a very attractive balance and harmony. This blending skill is characteristic of fine wines and the sign of a good winemaker. **Montcabrer** is a fine wine, which might be even better blended with Giró, whose viscosity and heady, fruity aroma, could bring something to the party.

Since the wine would not come to the mountain, the mountain has come to the wine, because as the Koran says in Surat 93, "The Brightness":

I swear by the early hours of the day,
And the night when it covers with darkness.
Your Lord has not forsaken you, nor has He become displeased,
And surely what comes after is better for you than that which has gone
before.
And soon will your Lord give you so that you shall be well pleased.

And one is indeed well pleased with this **Montcabrer** come down to us from the mountain.

Website: www.vinsdelcomtat.com
Label: Montcabrer
Type: Vino de reserva
ABV: 13%
Grape: Cabernet Sauvignon
Approx. price: €24
Bodega: Vins del Comtat
Address: Calle de Turballos, 1-3, Polígono de l'Alcúdia, 03820 Cocentaina, Alicante
Tel: 965593194
Fax: 965593590
Email: info@vinsdelcomtat.com

Pago de los Balagueses:
The Knights' Seal
Vegalfaro, El Azagador (DO Utiel-Requena)

Pago de los Balagueses is a small estate on the slopes of Los Isidros al Cabriel, on which the owner, Rodolfo Valiente, cultivates 25 **hectares** of his favourite Tempranillo and Syrah grapes. Over the last few years in Valencia 89 **hectares** of Syrah have been planted in Alicante, 25 in Valencia and 35 in Utiel-Requena. Syrah is king in the Côtes du Rhône, where it makes great reds. In the nineteenth century it had the same status as Bordeaux does today and before that was much enjoyed by the eighteenth-century novelist Henry Fielding, as it is today by John le Carré and Frederick Forsyth (who had a fine collection in his villa at Ondara).

It came to Europe from Syria in the twelfth century at the hands of the Frankish knights returning from the Crusades. The Crusaders established a principality in Syria for the protection of pilgrims. There the Knights Hospitaller took and fortified a great castle twenty-five miles from Homs, the Krak des Chevaliers, of which T.E. Lawrence, before he became Lawrence of Arabia, wrote, "It is the best preserved and most wholly admirable castle in the world." The Krak des Chevaliers had wells, aqueducts, a mill, ovens, warehouses and a great wine cellar, enough to allow the Hospitallers to withstand a five-year siege, impressive even in today's era of massive architecture. It is awe-inspiring to see it standing gigantically on the plateau overlooking the plain. Between Homs and the Bekaa Valley in Lebanon there was a sea of Syrah, which the Knights Hospitaller learned to tend and to admire for the quality of the grapes, their colour, spicy aroma and mature taste. Syrah wines are the tastiest of all reds, which is the highest gastronomic praise.

The **Pago de los Balagueses** tinto 2001 is a voluptuous Syrah that has been blended with Tempranillo, to add sharpness. It was left on its lees in new oak barrels, and stirred occasionally to extract still greater aroma and flavour. Rodolfo then aged it in French, Hungarian and American oak (two white oaks and one red, a perfect combination) still on its lees, which requires the individual care of each barrel, and the result is an extraordinary red. Its aroma is a complex and rich scent of violets, truffles and spices, and in the mouth it tastes of ripe fruits (blackcurrants, blueberries and, redcurrants) against a harmoniously fragrant background of toasted wood.

Website: www.vegalfaro.com
Label: Pago de Los Balagueses 2001 tinto
Type: Crianza (9 months in barrel)
ABV: 13.8%
Grapes: Syrah (90%), Tempranillo
Approx. price: €10–12
Bodega: Viñedos & Bodegas Vegalfaro
Address: Carretera Ponton-Utiel km.3, El Azagador, 46340 Requena, Valencia
Tel: 962138140
Fax: 962138154
Email: Rodolfo@vegalfaro.com

Pago de Tharsys Selección:
The Perfect "Château"
Pago de Tharsys, Requena (DO Utiel-Requena)

A "château" or domaine is a wine establishment set up in France around a working bourgeois rural property. It is more grandly aristocratic in Bordeaux, and tends to be more of a smallholding in Burgundy and the Côtes du Rhône. In other regions they lean towards one or the other according to the patterns of land ownership, but they all share a single underlying concept. The "cru" (literally "growth") is produced by the vines of a winegrowing property (château or domaine), is vinified on the property, is developed there and is bottled there. As such a château wine can only come from its own vineyards – and not just in a specific year, but every year. This created the best winegrowing and winemaking culture, and a system of standards that was the basis of the idea of the "**Denominación de Origen**" in Spain. **Pago de Tharsys** is the perfect château (see page 12). It is owned by Vicente García, a thoroughbred winemaker who has been involved with various significant Valencian wine projects (he was a founder of Torre Oria wines and the first technical director of **Covibex** [see page 8]), and the property stands on the main road between Requena and San Antonio. There is a beautiful restored old Valencian country "**alquería**", together with a lake that adds a sense of calm and beauty. Everything about **Pago de Tharsys** suggests nobility, even its name, which refers to the Greek Tharsys who according to legend founded Requena in 1531 BC. In **Pago de Tharsys** there are 12 **hectares** of Merlot, Cabernet Franc, Bobal and Tempranillo for red wine, and an interesting Albariño white. Vicente, who is an unusually determined winemaker, has developed this project to make fine wine on the strength of his passion for wine and his hardheaded love of this winemaking country, which he expresses methodically and meticulously in his search for excellence. He reminds me of Norberto Jorge, the best and most creative chef produced in the Valencia region, and his constant refrain: "What is quality? It is the absence of any weakness." And Vicente gives no indication of having any when it comes to winemaking, and to demanding the utmost seriousness in his profession. **Pago de Tharsys'** finest wine is **Selección** 2001, a mature "**alta expresión**" red wine of intense fragrance, with a scent of fruits of the forest, raspberry, vanilla and redcurrant. It is spicy, full of cinnamon and cloves, and a hint of

French toast in the aftertaste, very fine and very drinkable, showing the full ripeness of the grapes - each vine produces just 1.5 kilos. Harvesting is done at night, to maximize freshness. **Selección Pago de Tharsys** spends time in American and French oak, just enough to underpin its subsequent development in bottle until it achieves maturity. This is a wine with a great bouquet, a sublime red wine which conquers and seduces with its passion. As a wine for laying down, it can be drunk now or in a year's time, but it will keep for many years.

Website: www.pagodetharsys.com
Label: Selección tinto 2001
Type: vino de guarda, 11 months in barrel
ABV: 14%
Grapes: Cabernet Franc, Merlot
Approx. price: €26–28
Bodega: Pago de Tharsys
Address: Paraje de Fuencaliente s/n., Ctra. N-III, Km. 274, 46340 Requena, Valencia
Tel: 962303354
Fax: 962329000
Email: pagodetharsys@pagodetharsys.com

Porta Regia:
A "Cru" from Vinalopó
Valle del Carche, El Pinós (DO Valencia)

The Monastrell grape that has been grown in Alicante for the best part of 650 years is one of the oldest varieties in Spain. Red wines made from this grape have always been robust, dense, high in alcohol and full-bodied. Their colour and strength made them sought-after throughout Europe. Exports from this southern part of the Comunidad Valenciana provided revenue and prestige for centuries. But people's taste in wine changes, as it has done always. It was only ten years ago that the Riojans thought they were on top of the world, then the "**alta expresión**" reds appeared and the market changed with them. If this happened, it was because people were enjoying a different kind of red wine. In the late 1970s Alicante began to move towards a more modern style of wine. Whenever this happens, people start advocating tearing up vineyards and planting new varieties, which apparently produce the last word in wine elsewhere, but then they come up against this soil and this climate. That is why it is sensible to work with the virtues of Monastrell, which clearly had room for improvement, along the lines required by contemporary tastes. History marches on, making fools of us, and the "**alta expresión**" reds which are all the rage do not need to bypass the good old Monastrell grape after all. It turns out that modern technology, taking advantage of the ripeness that the grape achieves and the aromatic quality of the grape skins, its dense spiciness, enables the production of exactly these kinds of wines from our Monastrell. This is what **Valle del Carche**, a modern bodega with 125 **hectares** under vine, aimed for: to make a "grand cru" wine in Vinalopó. Located at the bottom of Sierra del Carche Nature Park, in El Pinós, this château works its own vineyards, producing a range of single varietal red wines, a **crianza** and a **reserva**: **Domus** (see page 40). But the outstanding wine is **Porta Regia** Monastrell, which is not only top quality, but a bargain at the price. **Bodegas Valle del Carche**, on its La Alberquilla property, grows Monastrell, Tempranillo, Cabernet Sauvignon, Syrah and Merlot for the reds, and Sauvignon Blanc and Chardonnay for its **Vaguada** and **Portichuelo** whites, which are full of fruit, but also redolent of heat like the wines from Kruger in Cape Town.

    Porta Regia Monastrell is a rich red wine, with plenty of spice: cinnamon and cloves; and fruit: cassis, cherry and ripe plum. It is full in the mouth, with a hint of liquorice, and an almost honeyed aftertaste, a wine to go with any part of a meal, even pudding. This is a red wine that can be kept for five or six years, improving all the time, but it will be at its best in late 2007.

Website: www.valledelcarche.es
Label: Porta Regia 2003
Type: tinto joven
ABV: 13%
Grape: Monastrell
Approx. price: €5–7
Bodega: Valle del Carche
Address: Paseo de la Constitución, 76 A, 03650 Pinoso, Alicante
Tel: 965978349
Fax: 965978060
Email: info@valledelcarche

Raspay:
Classic Alicante
Bodegas Primitivo Quiles, Monòver (DO Alicante)

"**C**lassic adj. 1. Of the first class, of the highest rank or importance; approved as a model; standard, leading" (*Oxford English
Dictionary*). This definition is appropriate for the great Alicante red wine,
Raspay from **Bodegas Primitivo Quiles** (see page 62) in Monòver,
made from Monastrell. Grown for 700 years in the Alicante "**huerta**",
from where it spread to the Vinalopó hinterland, the Monastrell grape
has always been notable for its colour, strength and stability. This red varietal is the standard-bearer for Alicante wines, much criticized when the
preferred Spanish taste was for anorexic and ovely acidic Rioja. Although
other wines from the country's peripheral wine regions had a lot going for
them, it made no difference, they were roundly criticized, ignored or sys-
tematically snubbed. Rioja and Spain were one and the same. But things
change, and in the late 1980s a new style of wine began to hold sway, one
in which the Mediterranean Monastrell stood out. The qualities of body,
spicy fruit, low acidity, roundness and sweet tannins were now perceived
by consumers as virtues of the best wines, and so again their worth was
justly proclaimed. From Priorat to Corsica, New Zealand to Alicante,
Languedoc to California, "**alta expresión**" wines are the wines of the
twenty-first century, and so the wheel turns, and those red wines of the
Mediterranean that ruled the roost from the Renaissance to the neoclassical era, and were looked on askance from the time of the Industrial
Revolution, emerge again – the most natural wines of all.

The red generosity of the Monastrell and the dry climate of Alicante's
Vinalopó valley are at the root of the great qualities of this red **Raspay**
that **Primitivo Quiles** makes with patience and precision. He makes a
few thousand bottles when he chooses a vintage, since **Raspay Tinto
Brut** is not made year in year out. It is aged in American and French oak,
and the end result is a mature, rounded, spicy red, ideal for partnering
meat and rice dishes (the magnificent Valle del Carxe paella is the perfect
dish to enjoy it with – see page 41). **Raspay** comes in at 14% ABV but
you would never know, as the great wines, even at this level of alcohol by
volume, offer an agreeably clean alcoholic punch, the result of a slow and
controlled production process. **Bodegas Primitivo Quiles** make other
interesting wines, the white **Cono 4** is quite some wine, and a **Fondillón**

that retains in the swollen bellies of its casks the maternal memory of a time when no one made it. There is also one of the best dessert wines in the world, up there with the great Ports and the all but lost wines from the Malaga mountains: **Gran Imperial** (see page 62). Primitivo Quiles is not only a great wine man who has maintained the Alicante tradition against all comers, he is also a good man. When you drink his wines and visit his bodega, remember what the Roman said: "Vinum animi speculum" ("Wine is the mirror of the soul"). Here we see this winemaker's reflected.

Website: www.primitivoquiles.com
Label: Raspay Brut
Type: Tinto crianza
ABV: 14%
Grape: Monastrell
Approx. price: €8–9
Bodega: Primitivo Quiles
Address: calle Major 4-6, 03640 Monòver, Alicante
Tel: 9659470 099
Fax: 966960235
Email: info@primitivoquiles.com

San Leandro:
Malvasía Communion Wine
La Baronía de Turís, La Ribera Alta (DO Valencia)

The highest-selling wine from the Valencia **DO** is the Communion wine from **Cooperativa de Turís** (see page 10). There isn't a diocese in Spain without a parish that buys this blessed Malvasía. Closely followed by the **Mistela** in terms of sales, it is an advance raiding party into the Spanish market on behalf of the rest of the wines from the Valencia **DO**, who need an institutional strategy from this body along the lines of those deployed by Ribera del Duero and Somontano, so that restaurant wine lists include a Valencia in the way they now have a Penedès or a Rueda. Wine is hugely symbolic in Christianity. The first Christians in Judea came from an already ancient wine culture, given that it passed from Sumeria, the birthplace of wine, to ancient Israel – this entire fertile crescent was a vast vineyard. Every religion has tried to influence what its believers eat and drink for reasons of ideology (doctrine) and politics (liturgy), be this Islam's protection of the health of the faithful in avoiding the risk of trichinosis from eating pork, or the discipline of the faith expressed in Christianity's Lenten fasting.

An Irish priest once said while he was drinking Bushmills whiskey (from Europe's oldest distillery): "All religions are good if drunk in moderation." Amen. As they say in deepest Somerset, "Blessed are those who can fast on Good Friday." But these food-related rites and disciplines have also given rise to good and delicious dishes, such as the "arròs caldòs de col y sepia" (cabbage and cuttlefish with rice) of the fishermen in Cabanyal, recovered as a restaurant dish – though it had never left the home table – by Valencia's Restaurante La Rosa in 1984, and presented with sacramental reverence to the late food writer Eugenio Domingo, Ignacio Medina – editor of the recipes of the world collection created by *El País* newspaper – and yours truly. The plate received our blessing and was included in the menu, from where it was copied by other restaurants. Another example is the **San Leandro** Communion wine, because as Vicente Riera, the founder and director of this cooperative, points out, the Fathers want a well-made wine. Being well-made is the first requirement for a Communion wine, which should be natural, quite full in the mouth and have a good level of alcohol. It should reflect the nature of the soil and be itself a good deed, as it is made for a good cause.

San Leandro, a pure Malvasía wine, is very aromatic, clean on the palate and deliciously full in the mouth. **San Leandro** can be bought for an eminently fair price at this good cooperative and eaten with sardines with eggs and onions like the fishermen of this coast. In Valencia's maritime El Cabanyal they say "Pel maig, sardina a la brassa i vi a la tassa" ("In May, sardine grilled and wine cup filled"). **San Leandro** fulfils the Knights Templar's requirement for a knight, to do good and do it well, something that the Catholic Church needs as much of as anyone in these times, beginning with more Christian charity to those believers with whom it disagrees. Let us drink to loving thy neighbour and the respect for their beliefs and the gods to which they pray, in the hope that an ecumenical humanism, even if this turns out to be secular, comes about. Otherwise the words of Abu'l-Ala-Al-Ma'arri will be proved true, though as yet they are but a half-truth: "The world holds two classes of men – intelligent men without religion, and religious men without intelligence."[1]

Website: www.baroniadeturis.es
Label: San Leandro 2004
Type: sweet white
ABV: 15%
Grape: Malvasía
Approx. price: €3–4
Bodega: La Baronía de Turís, Coop. V.
Address: Ctra. Godelleta, 22, 46389 Turís, Valencia
Tel: 962526011
Fax: 962527282
Email: acalvet@baroniadeturis.es

NOTES

[1] Abu'l-Ala-Al-Ma'arri (973–1057) was a blind Arab philosopher, poet and writer who was critical of Islam and religions in general.

Sanfir:
Lady Syrah, England Made Me
Casa del Pinar, Los Cojos (DO Utiel-Requena)

nglish weather has not made historically for good wine – Tacitus wrote of the inclement autumns, "The sky is overcast with continual rain and cloud, but the cold is not severe."[1] As a consequence, the British made a virtue of necessity and became the most discerning wine consumers and connoisseurs (the list of wine-tasting sages is extraordinary: Jancis Robinson, Michael Broadbent, Oz Clarke, Jan Read, and many more). They also emerged as creators and shapers of great wine styles, such as Bordeaux, Port, Sherry and Champagne. Without British involvement these wines would lack their distinctiveness and their quality. Britons were also involved in the planting of Syrah grapes, originally from Syria and Lebanon, on the banks of the Rhone where they produce extraordinary wines. My own initiation into the mysteries of Syrah came when I was having dinner with the cigar king, Zino Davidoff, at the Lion d'Or restaurant overlooking Lake Geneva. My host recommended a Lebanese wine – Château Kefraya – the purest essence of Syrah from the motherlode, the Bekaa valley. Few wines have made such an impression on me. I was seduced by the elegant yet potent blend of aromas and a wild, mature, sweet spiciness. I thought of Davidoff when I first came to taste the **Sanfir crianza** from **Casa del Pinar**. This is a small "château" which also incorporates some charming **casas rurales**. It is owned by Philip Diment and Ana Castillo, an Englishman and his Spanish wife, who moved to the Mediterranean having owned some of London's first and finest tapas restaurants.

Production is low, 25,000 bottles of their **crianza** and **reserva** all told. The aroma is dense and combines the scent of raspberries, blackberries and blackcurrants. There are added notes of vanilla and cinnamon alongside the exquisite sweetness of mature tannins achieved by constant stirring of the lees. **Maceration**, in new 300- and 400-litre oak barrels, follows the best contemporary practice as carried out in the Napa Valley, Priorat and Hawkes Bay. All this brings us a red wine of rare elegance, maturity, suppleness and vigour. This is a wine which is capable of holding its own against wines of its type from anywhere in the world, as is indicated by the fact that to date all the **Casa del Pinar** wines that have been entered in competition have garnered awards, including bronze and silver medals in the International Wine Challenge in London.

Website: www.casadelpinar.com
Label: Sanfir 2001
Type: crianza
ABV: 14%
Grapes: Syrah, Tempranillo, Merlot, Cabernet Sauvignon, Bobal
Approx. price: €10–12
Bodega: Casa del Pinar
Address: Carretera Los Isidros-Caudete Km 7, Los Cojos, 46354 Valencia
Tel: 962139120
Fax: 962 139 129
Email: diment@telefonica.net

NOTES

[1] Publius Cornelius Tacitus (55–117) was one of the most important ancient Roman historians. This observation is from *The Life and Death of Julius Agricola*, a biography of his father-in-law Agricola, Roman general and governor of the province of Britannia from 78–84 AD.

Santa Rosa:
A Multicultural Reserva
Enrique Mendoza, L'Alfàs del Pi (DO Alicante)

The great Wilbur Smith has said that as far as wine is concerned, what is sacred in France may not be so in the Transvaal. This is the basis of the new winemaking countries: South Africa, New Zealand, Australia, Chile and the United States, who have inherited European grape varieties and the full range of wine styles. One only has to see the grape harvest festivals in Napa Valley or Cape Town, which are like festivals of nations. The mixture has enriched their wines to help them rank among some of the best in the world, and this is exactly what José ("Pep") Mendoza in his bodega, **Enrique Mendoza**, in L'Alfàs del Pi.

The defenders of multiculturalism should seek out his wines. Pep is a modern winemaker with a broad vision. All his wines are made from his own vines and his watchword is that the best wine comes from the best vines. He grows Moscatel, Chardonnay, Cabernet Sauvignon, Merlot, Syrah, Pinot Noir, Petit Verdot and Monastrell. These make the wines of Bordeaux, Burgundy and the Côtes du Rhône, and also Alicante. With these grapes he makes an exquisite range of whites, reds, an outstanding dessert wine (**Dolç de Mendoza**) and a Moscatel de La Marina **Mistela**.

Pep is a master. Blending two, three or four grape varieties is difficult enough, but making a red out of two different styles is a real winemaking challenge. Mendoza meets it brilliantly with his extraordinary **Santa Rosa Reserva** 1999, made with Cabernet Sauvignon, Merlot and Syrah. The first two are the classic Bordeaux grapes, while Syrah makes the mature reds of the Côtes du Rhône. Bringing them together is a sensible enough idea for a good winemaker (which Pep is), but it requires special effort in the winery. **Santa Rosa** is first given six months in new American oak barrels and then a further ten months in French oak barrels from the Alliers forests. Alliers oak enhances oxidation, and the wood has the greatest ageing capacity of all the oak regions of central France. The end result is an extraordinary "reserve" with scents of vanilla, raspberry and green pepper, with a touch of ripe plum, vigour, toast, a smooth but sharp finish, and an astringency and acidity that make it ideal for laying down. This combination shows us that we are dealing with a man of culture and amiability (he has learned more from his travels than from schooling). The multiculturalism in his mixture of the exotic and the homegrown brings to mind a slogan of the movement which he embodies: "Think global, act local!"

Website: www.bodegasmendoza.com
Label: Santa Rosa red 1999
Type: Reserva (16 months in barrel)
ABV: 14%
Grapes: Cabernet Sauvignon, Merlot, Syrah
Approx. price: €18–20
Bodega: Enrique Mendoza
Address: Partida del Romeral s/n. L'Alfàs del Pi 03580, Alicante
Tel/Fax: 965 888 639
Email: bodegas-mendoza@bodegasmendoza.com

Solo:
Syrah
Dominio de Aranleón, Los Marcos (DO Utiel-Requena)

The Syrah "boulevard", a strip that runs from Requena to the Rambla de la Albosa in Los Isidros, is not only where the greatest quantity of this grape is grown in the Valencia region, but also where it achieves the highest quality. The soil and the climate of El Azagador, El Derramador, Los Marcos, Casa lo Alto, Los Cojos and Los Isidros are why this grape does so well in Utiel-Requena. The land is similar to the Syrian plain between the Bekaa Valley and Homs where the grape is originally from: the same latitude and the same distance from the Mediterranean Sea.

The **Dominio de Aranleón** bodega is in Los Marcos, under the spiritual and cultural direction of one of those people in love with wine and gastronomy – Emiliano García, owner of the splendid Casa Montaña tavern in old Cabanyal down near the sea in Valencia, is someone whose love of winemaking has turned him into a master of the subject. He has shown this in Casa Montaña and he is doing it again with the wines of **Aranleón**, with the help of Diego Fernández and María Sancho.

Aranleón's red **Solo** is a wine of 14% ABV made from almost equal quantities of Syrah, Tempranillo and Bobal, a well-judged blend when you think of the astringency and longevity of these varieties and their ripening cycles, which has given rise to so many great wines in California, South Africa, New Zealand, Corsica and the Languedoc. Aged for twelve months in 225-litre barrels of Hungarian and French oak (Alliers), there is a magnificent harmony between the wood tannins and the sweet ripeness of the grapes, and it has a lovely blood-red colour. The natural astringency of the Tempranillo and the Bobal grapes has been tamed, the first thanks to its characteristic structure in the mouth along with the residual sugar from the Syrah, and the Bobal thanks to its mature density, and since it is from old vines with a rugged undergrowth that has helped turn the grapes into divine berries.

Solo has one great virtue: its balance of taste and aroma. **Solo**'s bouquet is everlasting, elegant, dense and very smooth, like a "grand cru". This small, manageably-sized bodega with its limited production is one of the stars of Mediterranean winemaking thanks to the achievement of style and definition in its wines, a quality that is hard to identify but which is much missed when it is not present. That style that makes you fall in love with a particular wine as celebrated by W.B. Yeats, one of my favourite Irishmen:

> Wine comes in at the mouth
> And love comes in at the eye;
> That's all we shall know for truth
> Before we grow old and die.
> I lift the glass to my mouth,
> I look at you, and I sigh.[1]

Emiliano's culture and love of well-made wine underpin that quality behind **Solo** and the other wines from **Aranleón**. **Solo** is a wine that is there to be drunk, it is at its peak, drinking it is like being in the arms of a mature woman, all sensual pleasure and experience, with the elegance and the warm generosity of what comes naturally. **Solo**, a true luxury within our reach whose blood-red colour is truly Dionysian: a wine to inspire the soul and keep up the body's health and strength.

Website: www.aranleon.com
Label: Solo 2003
Type: Tinto reserva
ABV: 14%
Grapes: Syrah, Tempranillo, Bobal
Approx. price: €10–12
Bodega: Dominio de Aranleón
Address: Los Marcos, 46310 Requena, Valencia
Tel: 963631640
Fax: 963900481
Email: vinos@aranleon.com

NOTES

[1] William Butler Yeats, "A Drinking Song" (1916).

Terreta Rosé:
Essence of Place
Bodega Bocopa, Petrer (DO Alicante)

Monastrell, the Alicante grape par excellence, is true to its Mediterranean character in its prolific output. This grape produces red wines, as well as **Fondillón**, the legendary historic wine of Alicante, and some exquisite rosés. I have always stuck to the idea of using red grapes to make rosé wines, though in the 1980s there were areas, not Alicante and Utiel-Requena, where they insisted on making bad rosés by blending red and white wines. The rules allowed it, most of Spain's production was white and by blending these with lighter reds, a commercial product could be obtained, though one lacking gastronomic or vinous virtues. This did not change with Spain's entry into the EEC in 1985, because a seedy moratorium was negotiated which allowed the practice to continue, though not for export.

The confidence of those bodegas that stuck by the excellence and generosity of their genuine rosés, along with the steadfastness of regulatory authorities in promoting these wines to protect their heritage, for once enabled the good and sound to drive out the poor and counterfeit. A model of excellence in this respect is **Bocopa** from Vinalopó with their exquisite rosé, **Terreta Rosé**. The cooperative is well-known for its outstanding white wine, **Marina Alta**, and the modern reds **Marqués de Alicante**, as well as **Fondillón Alone**. This prince among cooperatives is a strategic undertaking by the **Generalitat** in the Vinalopó area. The end result has been highly positive, resulting in the overall modernization of the local wines, and equipping it for the marketplace.

Terreta Rosé is a young, intensely fruity rosé made from the Monastrell grape, with a bouquet of fresh strawberries and a startlingly brilliant colour. It is easy to drink, full in the mouth with good body, as if there was residual fructose. A rosé is made by separating the juice of the grape from the skins ("el sangrado"), just hours after the pressed grapes have been placed in the containers for maceration and fermentation. When the separation is carried out the grape must that pours out of the containers is a living nectar, bright red and headily aromatic, the smell is all about us, the virgin essence of wine, as if we were in the presence of the very spirit of wine. Every time I have made a rosé I have been reminded of "The Wine Ode" by Umar Ibn al-Farid:[1]

Purity not water,
subtlety not air,
light but not fire,
spirit without body.

Terreta Rosé is the spirit of wine and the essence of a Mediterranean land where the rosé expresses a festive way of seeing life, and a hedonistic enjoyment of its beauty. **Terreta Rosé** is a wine to enjoy in summertime, lighter than a red and to be drunk cooler (always an advantage in this climate) and it has more body than a white wine – the red for drinking in summer is rosé.

Website: www.bocopa.com
Label: Terreta Rosé 2003
Type: rosé
ABV: 12.5%.
Grape: Monastrell
Approx. price: €3–4
Bodega: Bocopa
Address: Paraje Les Pedreres, Autovía A-31 Km 200-201, 03610 Petrer, Alicante
Tel: 966950489
Fax: 966950406
Email: info@bocopa.com

NOTES

[1] The Sufi poet and scholar Umar Ibn al-Farid (1181–1235) is regarded as one of the great mystic poets.

Vall de Xaló:
Black Mistela
Coop. Virgen Pobre, La Marina Alta (DO Alicante)

Not all Moscatels are **Mistelas**, nor are all **Mistelas** made from Moscatel. The technique of adding alcohol to grape juice to interrupt fermentation is so ancient that there is no wine it has yet to be tried with. The aim of this "mistelización" is to make a wine that is longlasting, sweet and stable (due to the presence of the added alcohol). It has been tried with Malvasía, Grenache Blanc (also known as Peluda), Merlot, Garnacha (yes, a red **Mistela**!), even with Gewürztraminer, though that is not so strange given that it is an aromatic variety. Félix Cuartero, professor and leading light of the Requena Wine School, a fine man and a wonderful winemaker, made a Gewürztraminer **Mistela** in the school winery that is the best I have ever tasted.

Another outstanding **Mistela** is Maestrat made by the Alcalà de Xivert cooperative with Grenache Blanc. Manuel Vázquez Montalbán (see page 51) broadcast its existence to gourmets in his novel *Southern Seas*, in which Fuster (the character who recommends this elixir), Carvalho – the great detective – and Biscuter, his sidekick, make short work of a carafe. **The Virgen Pobre de Xaló** cooperative has such an efficient marketing director that they sell most of their output in the bodega itself (if the virgin is poor it is not as a result of low sales). There isn't a Scandinavian, Anglo-Saxon, German, Celt or Frenchman living on the Valencian coast who isn't a regular client. This cooperative in the Valle de Xaló (which is also a top-class gastronomic centre) makes a dessert wine, a **Mistela**, a good **crianza** red – **Duquesa de Almodóvar** – an old-fashioned vermouth, whites made from Moscatel and genuine rosés from Garnacha. They also make a distinctive and magnificent red with Giró (as the Garnacha grape is known hereabouts) following their own particular method. In some years in this valley excess humidity gives rise to the *botrytis cinerea* fungus – the very same that lies behind the renowned Sauternes. The winemaking miracle that takes place is that this fungus, instead of destroying the grape, dries it out, turning it almost into a raisin, and the wine made from these grapes is a mature red, with a rich array of aromas (redcurrants, raspberries, blueberries, strawberries, plums), an extraordinary wine that unfortunately does not occur every year. The red **Mistela** of Vall de Xaló is a cultural curiosity, with the astringency of a young red and the sweetness of fortified grape juice. It is ideal for sitting around drinking at the end of a meal. It is even better with a bit of age, not unlike a vintage Port (or a Late Bottled Vintage), and we can all benefit from its mature richness.

website: www.bodegaxalo.com
Label: Vall de Xaló
Type: Red Mistela
ABV: 15%
Grape: Giró (Garnacha)
Approx. price: €3–4
Bodega: Coop. Virgen Pobre
Address: Carretera Xaló-Alcalalí s/n, 03727 Xaló, Alicante
Tel: 966480034
Fax: 966480808
Email: info@bodegaxalo.com

Vegalfaro Crianza:
A Modern Blend
Bodegas Vegalfaro, El Azagador (DO Utiel-Requena)

The planting of French varietals in the Valencian **Denominaciones de Origen** has given rise to the suggestion that we might be seen as almost a New World wine producer, like South Africa, New Zealand or California, in stylistic if not in geographical terms. Despite a wine culture going back thousands of years and a very identifiable wine identity, having as many as ten northern grape varieties has led to our developing a new wine culture, one brought about by the presence in the region of the following: Syrah, Cabernet Sauvignon, Cabernet Franc, Merlot, Pinot Noir, among others. These varietals belong to the three main winegrowing areas in France: Côtes du Rhône, Bordeaux and Burgundy, where the styles are set in stone. But here they are not, and delicious blends are also to be made from our local grapes, so prospects are good.

Vegalfaro is a fully-furbished modern bodega that is the epitome of a well-run small business. It makes wine from grapes grown in its own vineyards, dotted about in the "pagos" of La Muela, Alfaro and Balagueses in the Requena district. They are very much "**finca**" wines. It produces delightful rosés, refined and elegant whites, especially their "**barrel-fermented**" white wine, and a magnificent Syrah, **Pago de los Balagueses** (see page 92) whose density and correctness remind me of the great Lebanese wines: Château Kefraya and Château Musar. Rodolfo Valiente, director and winemaker, makes a modern single estate wine: **Vegalfaro** 2003, using Syrah, Tempranillo, Merlot and Garnacha, a blend that would be outlandish in France and yet here seems just right. Rodolfo is a winemaker with an enquiring mind, he gave up the law in order to make good wine, and this he has achieved, through the qualities Don Quixote identified as necessary for a different kind of composition: "senor bachelor, there is need of great judgment and a ripe understanding." **Vegalfaro** is a single estate wine, the very estate that encircles the bodega. It has been aged for nine months in French and Hungarian white oak barrels with a little red American oak from Missouri. It comes in at 13.8%, and there is a depth on the nose as a result of the **maceration** of good, healthy, ripe and clean skins, which offer that elegant cinnamon and vanilla spice. It is also a delicious wine, with a lively redcurrant aroma.

In the mouth it is dry with plenty of tannins, noble in its straightforwardness. It is a wine that tastes of wine, with an aftertaste that leaves a lingering pleasant memory, of tannins from new barrels, and the ripeness of the Garnacha, Syrah and Merlot grapes. The role of Tempranillo in this blend is to contribute longevity, as the grape's astringency helps to unite and preserve the qualities of the other grape varieties. It is a red wine which one ought to go out and buy, which makes me think of a special breed of people to whom we owe more than we think: wine merchants. Winemakers can make fine wines, but they then have to be sold. In their honour, I quote Omar Khayyam's magnificent tribute in the *Rubaiyat* (see page 23): "Well, I wonder often what the Vintners buy One half so precious as the stuff they sell."

Website: www.vegalfaro.com
Label: Vegalfaro 2003
Type: Tinto crianza de Finca
ABV: 13.8%
Grapes: Syrah, Tempranillo, Garnacha, Merlot
Approx. price: €6–7
Bodega: Vegalfaro
Address: Ctra. Pontón-Utiel, km. 3, 46340 Requena, Valencia
Tel: 962138140
Fax: 962138154
Email: Rodolfo@vegalfaro.com

Verderón Chardonay:
Glamour and Elegance
Casa del Pinar, Los Cojos (DO Utiel-Requena)

The whole place emanates a perfumed sense of vivacity and freshness. Philip Diment and Ana del Castillo, the owners of **Casa del Pinar**, a small bodega in Los Cojos near Requena, impressed lovers of good wine with their **Sanfir crianza** (see page 102) and **Casa del Pinar Reserva**, and have now produced a new delight, **Verderón**, made with Chardonnay.[1]

The 2004 harvest was a pure pearl, the sheer essence of the grape, fermented in French oak barrels, magnificent barrels whose embrace saw the merging of the heady aroma – practically a perfume – with the silky mature taste into something divine. This wine also achieves true beauty in its brilliantly clear topaz hue. Philip and Ana, the creators of these wines, show their good taste in all that they do, from making their wine to running their "**casas rurales**" attached to the bodega. These are elegant and comfortable houses that might have stepped straight from the pages of *Country Life*.

Chardonnay, first planted in Utiel-Requena twenty-five years ago, comes from the north of France, where it is used in the making of the great Burgundies and Champagnes. It is a white grape, noble, elegant and refined. It is in barrel that the best Chardonnays are achieved, revealing their great virtue, their subtle and persistent aromas.

The range of aromas creates a perfumed feeling of vivacity and freshness, but also an attractive and alluring maturity. I tasted this wine in the final moment of its alcohol fermentation, before it began the malolactic fermentation, and I was seduced by its enchanting sparkle, its heady aroma and its silky mouth. We stand before a great Chardonnay which will stand out among the legions of Chardonnays which have been made in Spain. On tasting it a few months later, this wine had enriched its bouquet further with an aftertaste of buttered toast with a hint of spices (cinnamon and cloves).

Philip and Ana have also achieved something special with this white wine, as well as the usual Chardonnay aromas: hints of pineapple, and night jasmine and nuts (walnut and hazelnut) which is reminiscent of the best Chablis from the south of Burgundy. Such a wine, with all respect to its very wineness, is a nectar that gives lasting pleasure to the eyes, the nose and the mouth. This **Verderón** seduces with a smile, as its makers understand the nature of a great wine and how not to overdo things. The lines of this wine bring to mind St John of the Cross: "Con su sola figura prendados los dejó con su hermosura" ("With his image alone, clothed them in beauty").[2]

> **Website:** www.casadelpinar.com
> **Label:** Verderón 2004
> **Type:** Barrel-fermented white
> **ABV:** 13%
> **Grapes:** Chardonnay
> **Approx. price:** €10–11
> **Bodega:** Casa del Pinar
> **Address:** Los Cojos, 46340 Requena, Valencia
> **Tel:** 9621391 2
> **Fax:** 962139121
> **Email:** diment@telefonica.net

NOTES

[1] Since this was first written, Verderón has been made with Sauvignon Blanc rather than Chardonnay.

[2] St John of the Cross (1542–1591) was a Spanish mystic and Carmelite friar and priest. He was a major figure in the Catholic Reformation.

Vermut Vittore:
A Blast from the Past
Cherubino Valsangiacomo, Chiva (DO Valencia)

In Spain, largely as a result of the Riojans' ceaseless efforts to associate wine-drinking with status value rather than concentrating on the actual qualities of a given wine, vermouths have never received their due recognition. But the production and nurturing of a vermouth requires a high quality bodega, with the necessary winemaking know-how and tradition. When Spain was dominated by a Castilian–Andalusian oligarchy, Rioja and Sherry were the most prestigious wines. The offerings of the Mediterranean periphery (vermouths and sweet **Mistelas**) were of a different type and were drinks for the common people, and so have not enjoyed the reputation that they deserve. This is not the case in France and Italy. Remember Stanley Kramer's "The Secret of Santa Vittoria" (1969), with Anthony Quinn and the magnificent Virna Lisi, in which a village hides its wine to avoid its appropriation by the Nazis – the wine they're concealing is vermouth. These countries appreciate the range and diversity of winemaking, they know that vermouth is part of their heritage and there is prestige in making it. They have not forgotten the fundamentals – that vermouth is the oldest of the wines made by man, brought to us from the dawn of time, perhaps even at the hands of Jason and the Argonauts – its eternal verities expressed by Alcaeus of Mitylene (c. 625–c. 575 BC), "Wine, dear boy, and truth."[1] In the Middle Ages vermouth (from the German "Wermut", meaning wormwood) found sanctuary in the monasteries, the German Benedictines, as wise in matters of horticulture as in distilling, improved the traditional recipe. **Bodegas Valsangiacomo**, founded in the Swiss canton of Ticino 175 years ago and established in the port of Valencia over a century ago, combine tradition and wisdom. It is a family bodega currently run by the fifth generation. **Vermut Vittore** is made in the traditional way with herbs from the Mariola mountains between Alicante and Valencia, which are then **macerated** in distilled wine and water to achieve the concentrate, which is subsequently aged in old oak with red wine from the region. Valsangiacomo, a specialist in the subject, recalls at leisure vermouths from Carpano in Italy, Marseilles, and his own Torino-style red vermouth. He also makes one of the few authentic traditional **Mistelas**. Over the last decade, **Bodegas Valsangiacomo** has also successfully entered the modern fine wine market, and their **Castillo de l'Olleria**, **Selección de Otoño** and **Marqués de Caro** are appreciated across the European Union, Japan, the USA and Switzerland.

Website: www.cherubino.es
Label: Vermut Vittore
Type: Turin Vermouth (red)
ABV: 15%
Grapes: Bobal and Monastrell
Approx. price: €4–6
Bodega: Cherubino Valsangiacomo
Tel: 962510861
Email: cherubino@cherubino.es

NOTES

[1] Alcaeus (*c.*620–c550 BC) was a Greek lyric poet, born at Mytilene in Lesbos. The surviving fragments of his poems deal with politics, drinking and love.

Viña Bárbara Reserva:
A Victory for Cooperation
Covibex, Chiva (DO Valencia)

One of the best decisions ever made by Lluís Font de Mora when he was in charge of agriculture in the early days of the **Generalitat** after the Franco dictatorship, was the creation of first- and **second-grade cooperatives** in the central "**comarcas**", to make wine from the grapes of small villages who wanted to keep their winemaking identity and the tradition of their mini-cooperatives – places like Benicolet, Xiva, Los Campos, Valdobar – in the Vall d'Albaida, Alt Túria and Foia de Bunyol. In the '90s the Valencian wine sector was still very closed and polarized, and the project had its advocates and opponents, but with the help of like-minded individuals (though some were even more of a hindrance than the out-and-out opponents) the plan saw the light of day, and today **Covibex** is a modern cooperative that represents the best in Valencian cooperatives (see page 8).

Its **Viña Bárbara Reserva** is made with Cabernet Sauvignon and Tempranillo, two long-lived, tannic grape varieties that, after a year in American and French oak develop a more refined bouquet and give rise to a well-balanced wine, with some tannins from the barrel, but plenty of ripe fruit (raspberries and lychees) and spices (vanilla and cloves). **Covibex**, in addition to its modern installation, has Ana Soria, one of the finest Valencian winemakers, who makes a Sémillon from grapes grown in Xiva. As the soil and climate here are different to those in the grapes' principal home on the left bank of the Garonne in Bordeaux, this Semillon is an interesting aromatic white, not far removed from our local Moscatel wine. Though non-Valencian grape varieties have taken well to the region, their incomer status should be kept in mind, sixty years in the case of Tempranillo and thirty for Cabernet. The Mediterranean climate is kind to them, as the low levels of humidity make the ingenious cultivation methods of, say, Rioja and Bordeaux, unnecessary. So, **Covibex** and Ana Soria have chosen wisely with their blend, as the Cabernet Sauvignon is producing better wines than when it first arrived, and will be better still in thirty years. Originally, varieties like Cabernet Sauvignon, Cabernet Franc, Merlot, Pinot and Chardonnay were planted here because of their reputation (as Flaubert said in his *Dictionary of Received Ideas*, "The best is Bordeaux, as doctors ask for it"),[1] but time has shown that once adapted to this environment, they end up producing wines as distinctly Valencian as our own Monastrell, Bobal or Garnacha, in an excellent expatriate blend.

Website: www.anecoop.com
Label: 1997
Type: Tinto 12 months in barrel and 24 months in bottle.
ABV: 12.5%.
Grapes: Cabernest Sauvignon, Tempranillo
Approx. price: €9–11
Bodega: Covibex.
Address: Carretera N-III km 314, Chiva 46370, Valencia
Tel: 962522200
Fax: 96 252 2678
Email: covibex@covibex.com

NOTES

[1] Gustave Flaubert, *Le Dictionnaire des idées reçues* (1911–13, published posthumously) is a work collecting and satirizing the platitudes of the French society of the day.

Viña Lidón:
White Wine and Wood
Vera de Estenas, San Antonio (DO Utiel-Requena)

Barrels were originally used not for ageing, but for transport. Julius Caesar described how the Gauls used oak barrels, which he called "cupae". At that time wine was transported in amphoras, but these broke easily and affected both naval (ports and ships) and civil (bodegas, houses and taverns) structures. The Port of Ostia would fill up with the remains of broken amphoras and had to be dredged once a year. The oak cask solved this problem, as it could be used for transport, storage and as receptacles in taverns. They were also used for fermentation, as "lagares" (wine troughs) and "tinajas" (clay containers) were not always available.

Fermenting in barrel goes back thousands of years, then, for which we can thank the Gauls and the great oak forests of France. It was lucky that France was late to enter the race for the Americas, otherwise the forests of the Massif Central would no doubt have been cut down, as Spain's were. It is worth remembering that to make a triple-decker (plus bowsprit and prow) required 2,000 noble oak trees (over 150 years old and 100 feet high, amounting to 60 acres of forest). Today the cutting down of these trees in France is controlled by the state, and both on private and public land any felling of oaks is carried out only at the behest of the French forestry commission.

Thanks to these white oak barrels (Limousine, Alliers, Nevers and, when possible, Tronçais – the best of all) we get barrel-aged and **barrel-fermented** wines as fine as **Viña Lidón** from **Vera de Estenas**. The owner and winemaker, Félix Martínez, is the latest in an long-established Utiel-Requena wine dynasty. This bodega, one of the first to use international grape varieties, is set in Vera de Estenas, in Utiel, just beyond the railway line between Valencia and Madrid via Cuenca.

Viña Lidón is made with Chardonnay, fermented in barrel and emerging at 12.5% ABV, ideal for this type of wine. It is a translucent pale amber in colour. It has the nutty aroma characteristic of barrel-fermented wines (walnuts and hazelnuts), and is pure silk in the mouth (also typical of this type of wine). **Viña Lidón** is a very harmonious wine, with a potent but elegant structure and complexity. Félix Martínez also makes some excellent reds, including **Viña Mariola**, a red wine with legions of admirers, despite its limited production. My Latin, which is a long way from Julius Caesar's (whose pen was as mighty as his sword), is just about good enough to relish the etymology of words related to wine ("coupage" – blending – comes from "cupae"), and to say, like the Romans, "vinum lac senum" ("wine is old people's milk"), or rather wine keeps you young.

Website: www.veradeestenas.es
Label: Viña Lidón 2004
Type: Barrel-fermented white
ABV: 12.5%
Grape: Chardonnay
Approx. price: €7–9
Bodega: Vera de Estenas
Address: Finca Casa Don Angel, Paraje La Cabezuela, Ctra. N-III, km. 266, 46300 Utiel, Valencia
Tel: 962171141
Fax: 962174352
Email: estenas@veradeestenas.es

Viña Teulada:
A Mediterranean White
Coop. Sant Vicent Ferrer, Teulada (DO Alicante)

The Moscatel of Alexandria grape has been grown in the Valencia region for over 2,000 years. It is also known as Moscatel Romano, because the Romans brought it to western Europe, and as Moscatel de Valencia, because it was from here that it spread to the Roman provinces of Galia Narbonensis (Provence) and Betica (Andalusia). It is grown in nearly all the Valencian winemaking "**comarcas**", and produces the renowned **Mistela**, but over twenty years ago **Gutiérrez de la Vega** and the Cooperativa de Godelleta began making dry as well as sweet moscatel wines. Moscatel is one of the elite aromatic white grape varietals, along with Sémillon, Gewürztraminer, Riesling, Sauvignon Blanc, Chardonnay and Malvasía. Only the latter and Moscatel are Mediterranean, the others are from the European mainland, suggesting the capacity of the first two to produce aromatic, elegant and fresh wines.

The Mediterranean varietals have strong fruit aromas – of apricots, melons, bananas and other fruits. Moscatel is the most aromatic and distinctive of all. At wine-tastings, when discussing what a wine like **Viña Teulada** tastes of, the answer is always "Moscatel!" Not fruity or aromatic, or reminiscent of pears or pineapple, as with other wines, just Moscatel. The problem with making Moscatels is the high concentration of fructose, which after harvestin, as acidity levels fall and meet sugar levels on the rise, produces an almost sweet wine. That is why the bodegas that make this style of wine, whether sweet or dry, bring forward or delay harvesting to achieve either greater acidity and freshness, or sweetness, as required. One of the bodegas to have mastered this is **Bocopa** (see pages 70 and 108), with their famous **Marina Alta**, and **Viña Teulada** is in the same mould.

Viña Teulada is an aromatic white wine, with good fruit, lightness, a touch of acidity that veils its sweetness. Moscatel is a Mediterranean grape, which gives of its best near the sea, as in the terraces of Teulada, where it is wafted by the gentle sea breeze. Moscatel confirms what Alexander Henderson wrote in his great *The History of Ancient and Modern Wines* (Baldwin, Cradock and Joy, 1824), the first English-language book on winemaking ever printed, that wines should be harvested and drunk when the wind blows from the north. The **Teulada cooperative** (see page 74), which has a celebrated commitment to wine and the culture of wine, also produces a traditional **Mistela** (with grapes that have almost turned into raisins), another modern-style wine, and limited quantities of an artisanal vermouth.

Website: www.coop-santvicent.com
Label: Viña Teulada 2003
Type: Young white
ABV: 11.5%
Grape: Moscatel of Alexandria
Approx. price: €3–4
Bodega: Cooperativa Sant Vicent Ferrer de Teulada
Address: Avenida de Las Palmas,32 Teulada 03725, Alicante
Tel: 965740051
Fax: 965740489
Email: bodega@coop-santvicent.com

Viña Ulises:
Bloomsday in La Marina
Gutiérrez de la Vega, Parcent (DO Alicante)

A man's character is his destiny, and Felipe Gutiérrez de la Vega's was to become one of the best wine producers in this country (see page 16). From infancy we all follow a dream, this dream is a guide that allows us to find our real selves. After marriage to Pilar Sapena de Parcent he left his secure future (he was a naval officer) to devote himself to making wine in a locality where this activity was going through a bad patch. A few decades on he has created an extraordinary heritage. He modernized these wines, which did not even come under the protection of a **Denominación de Origen**. His wine changed the whole prospect. **Casta Diva Cosecha Miel** Moscatel is possibly the best white wine in the whole Mediterranean, and the **"vin doux naturel"** **Casta Diva Reserva Real** was chosen for the wedding of Prince Felipe and Leticia Ortiz, an excellent choice. **Casta Diva** has such elegance and smoothness, and such a natural scent of raisins, that it makes a perfect alternative to Sauternes to accompany foie gras, especially if this is from Périgord as served in L'Armeler Restaurant in Sagunto, where it is a speciality of the house. His white Moscatels – he has even made one, **Cavatina**, that is a "vino de aguja" (slightly sparkling) – are sensual and seductive, and are dedicated to his operatic passions: Maria Callas, Alfredo Kraus, Donizetti and Montserrat Caballé among others. For Valencian winemakers, Felipe is a great professional and a fine "bodeguero" who makes excellent wines. For the English artist Richard Hamilton,[1] Felipe is above all an artist, as he was previously for Camilo José Cela.[2]

He also makes distinctive red wines. **Tambourine Casta Diva** 2001, made with Giró de la Marina (Garnacha) and Monastrell, was chosen by the University of Wales for an international Classics Conference, and they still sing the praises of its bouquet in the valleys. Another dense, fragrant red that is wonderful on the palate is **Casta Diva Príncipe de Salina**, dedicated to Giuseppe di Lampedusa.[2] But the best is **Viña Ulises**, dedicated to Homer and James Joyce. I remember it from years ago, when he began production in a **"riu-rau"** in the vineyards of La Riba, making wine in oak barrels when no one else did, a man ahead of his time, and **Viña Ulises** was the first **"alta expresión"** red wine in

Spain. **Viña Ulises** is a Mediterranean red in the noblest sense of the word. It is made with Monastrell and Giró (Garnacha), as this wine works wonderfully in La Marina, which combines the features that best suit the grape, the microclimate of the Xaló, Alcalalí and Lliber valleys and the proximity of the Mediterranean are ideal for its cultivation. **Viña Ulises** is elegant on the palate, cosmopolitan but with a definite identity. Its refinement brings to mind a Saint-Emilion Grand Cru, while its nose, with its scent of ripe fruit (blueberries and redcurrants) and spices, is that of a Côtes du Rhône. **Viña Ulises** is a vigorous **crianza**, with a long life ahead of it. It is almost a "vin de garde", and will continue gradually to evolve and to improve. It certainly has something of Leopold Bloom about it, especially the scene in Dublin's National Maternity Hospital, evoking birth, life and the evolution of language. Felipe's friend Richard Hamilton created the Joycean label, conveying the different stages of gestation expressed by Joyce in this scene, as in all of *Ulysses*. As with **Viña Ulises**, which makes me think of Joyce's lines:

> O Ireland my first and only love
> Where Christ and Caesar are hand and glove![3]

Website: www.castadiva.es
Label: Viña Ulises 2000
Type: Tinto Crianza
ABV: 13.5%
Grapes: Giró (Garnacha), Monastrell
Approx. price: €18–20
Bodega: Gutiérrez de la Vega
Address: Canalejas 4, 03792 Parcent, Alicante
Tel: 966405266
Fax: 966405257
Email: info@castadiva.es

NOTES

[1] Richard Hamilton (born 1922) is a key figure in the British Pop Art movement.

[2] The Prince of Salina is the protagonist of Giuseppe di Lampedusa's novel, *The Leopard* (Feltrinelli, 1958).

3 James Joyce, "Gas from a Burner" (1912).

Lightning Source UK Ltd.
Milton Keynes UK
UKOW021851180912

199223UK00007B/3/A